# How to Smell a Rat

# Fisher Investments Press

Fisher Investments Press brings the research, analysis, and market intelligence of Fisher Investments' research team, headed by CEO and *New York Times* best-selling author Ken Fisher, to all investors. The Press covers a range of investing and market-related topics for a wide audience—from novices to enthusiasts to professionals.

## Books by Ken Fisher

*How to Smell a Rat*
*The Ten Roads to Riches*
*The Only Three Questions That Count*
*100 Minds That Made the Market*
*The Wall Street Waltz*
*Super Stocks*

### Fisher Investments Series

*Own the World*
Aaron Anderson
*20/20 Money*
Michael Hanson

### Fisher Investments On Series

*Fisher Investments on Energy*
*Fisher Investments on Materials*
*Fisher Investments on Consumer Staples*
*Fisher Investments on Industrials*

FISHER
INVESTMENTS
PRESS

# How to Smell a Rat

## The Five Signs of Financial Fraud

### Ken Fisher
with
Lara Hoffmans

**WILEY**

John Wiley & Sons, Inc.

Published by John Wiley & Sons, Inc., Hoboken, New Jersey.
Published simultaneously in Canada.

For general information on our other products and services or for technical support, please
contact our Customer Care Department within the United States at (800) 762-2974,
outside the United States at (317) 572-3993 or fax (317) 572-4002.

Wiley also publishes its books in a variety of electronic formats. Some content that appears
in print may not be available in electronic books. For more information about Wiley
products, visit our web site at www.wiley.com.

*Library of Congress Cataloging-in-Publication Data:*

Fisher, Kenneth L.

    How to smell a rat : the five signs of financial fraud / Ken Fisher with Lara W. Hoffmans.
       p.   cm. — (Fisher investments series)
    Includes bibliographical references and index.
    ISBN 978-0-470-52653-8 (cloth)
       1. Fraud—Prevention.   2. Commercial crimes.   3. Investments.   4. Swindlers
    and swindling.   I. Hoffmans, Lara.   II. Title.
  HV6691.F57 2009
  364.16'3—dc22

                                                2009021631

Printed in the United States of America

10  9  8  7  6  5  4  3  2  1

# Contents

# Acknowledgments

Both 2008 and early 2009 were very tough capital market environments. They were terrible times, made all the more so by the discovery, late in 2008 and early in 2009, of some pretty big, ugly, heinous financial frauds. Though scams are typically outed at and around bear market bottoms—and this was no different, just a bigger bear market hence bigger outing of scams—something struck me about the media coverage of all these scams. They were missing the very easy and obvious unifying element all the scams had in common that would make it simple and easy for investors to avoid being scammed. (I won't tell you here, you must read the book to find out.) And in that, I saw a book not only that I could write, but that I should write, and now was the time. To me, this was important—it was worth a bit of my time to get it out, fast.

And to get it out fast while keeping 100 percent focused on my day job required some major help, so I turned to Lara Hoffmans, who worked with me on both of my last two books. I described the book and gave her ideas, names to pursue and research, and a myriad of inputs. She then put together an organizational plan which, once blessed, she pursued in doing the heavy lifting in constructing an entire first draft of the book.

I am a writer—love writing and have for a long time. Pretty much in the small percentage of my life when I'm not directly working, I'm either putting time into my family or one of three hobbies. Writing is one of them. Now writing is mostly re-writing, editing yourself, seeing how you can say what you wanted to say but better, shorter, punchier, and with less words—and all that's fun for me. But books can also be a lot of work. But in this one Lara did most of the grunt-work heavy lifting, and I got to have most of the fun. So I really do have to acknowledge Lara for over-the-top contributions to making this book a reality. She did so on my last two books, but with each book she seems to pull off a greater portion of the total labor load.

Also special thanks are necessary to Dina Ezzat, from my firm's Content Management group. She helped out enormously in running down sources and citations, and generally helping with nit-picky tactical details. That helps tremendously and saves me endless time. Evelyn Chea, also in our Content group, always does a great job of copy editing our work and was no exception this time.

I also must thank Michael Hanson and Aaron Anderson, both very accomplished writers in their own right and senior members of our Content group. Though already carrying an impressive load of responsibilities, they helped by picking up the slack when I redirected Lara to help me on this book. And thanks too to Fab Ornani, who heads the Content group and does too many things for his own good, among them being our in-house web guru. Fab directed and load-balanced the whole group while I had Lara, Dina, and Evelyn distracted.

I also owe a debt of gratitude to both Marc Haberman, our Chief Innovation Officer; Molly Lienesch, our branding manager; and Tommy Romero, group vice president of marketing, who handled all the non-writing efforts that went into this book. I didn't have to do anything at all in this regard. And, of course, Fred Harring, Tom Fishel, and Nicole Gerrard gave the manuscript a close read for legal issues—which I appreciate immeasurably. I'd hate to be sued just for trying to prevent people from losing their money to a con artist.

As always, Jeff Herman, literary agent extraordinaire, contributed his views on what would make this book of interest to you. He keeps his hand on the pulse of book readers and has a much better sense of what you want than I ever could. And more than ever, I must thank the team I work with at John Wiley & Sons including David Pugh, Joan O'Neil, Nancy Rothschild, and Peter Knapp for their help. This is the first time with one of my books that I didn't come up with the title; they did. It is legendarily and notoriously difficult for book authors to get along with book publishers; but they make it easy.

Clients at my firm sometimes get irked, thinking I take time away from work for these books, which I should be spending on them. But I never do, never have. I always work a minimum 60-hour week—always have—and most weeks it's more like 70 hours. I indulge my writing hobby after that on weekends. As with any hobby, the release recharges me for my "day" job. Unfortunately, the person overwhelmingly who gets short changed when I do this is my wife of 38 years, Sherrilynn, who I never get to spend as much time with as I should and who is always patient with me as I exert myself on any of my hobbies. To her I always owe a debt of gratitude and particularly so when I launch off on writing which requires longer sustained bursts of energy than my redwoods hobbies.

Finally, thank you for taking time with this book. I've done five books before and had two *New York Times* best sellers. If even two of the five signs of financial fraud resonate in your head like a bestseller and keep you from being scammed by a con artist, having put the little time I did into this book will have been very worthwhile for me.

Ken Fisher
Woodside, CA

# Introduction

Imagine this:

Jim's a decent, hard-working, working stiff—frugal, with a nice nest egg. Between his job, family, a serious Saturday golf addiction, and some community commitments, he hasn't the time, know-how, or inclination for investing details. And there are so many confusing options—tens of thousands of mutual funds, thousands of money managers. Hedge funds. Brokerage products with confusing names. Too much! So he turns to friends for advice—like you might. Turns out his golf partner, boss, and a few fellow church members all invest with the same adviser—have for years—Mr. Big Time. They swear by him!

Big Time is pretty famous—held a big government post in the '80s. He manages several billion now, mostly for rich folks—way out of Jim's league. Big Time is so big, he's his own broker-dealer—Big-Time Portfolios, Inc. Jim's friends say Big Time never had a down year—not 1987, not in the 2000–2002 bear, and not the most recent bear. His returns look pretty darn stable—and after a few rough years, stability sounds good to Jim.

Jim's golf buddy fixes a meeting. Big Time's office is posh, including photos of Big Time with diverse celebrities. All of the last three Presidents. Brett Favre. The Pope. Bono. There's Big Time flying his private jet. Winning a regatta in his yacht. He does well—it shows. He's dripping with success.

Amazingly enough, when Jim comes to Big Time's office, Big Time himself meets Jim! (Though he makes it clear he's very busy and can't talk long.) Jim asks about performance—what's the strategy? BT explains: It's proprietary—even most staff aren't 100 percent privy to it—wouldn't want it to get out. If an employee left and took it outside—maybe gave the secret to a competitor—it would hurt Big Time's clients. Mr. B is earnest—he must protect existing clients. Jim feels bad insisting about knowing all this, but this is his life savings. BT hasn't got time to explain—it's complicated—involves option hedging RMBSs overlaid with swaps, some arbitrage, some playing volumes—which cuts the volatility, hence the consistency.

Jim's only ever bought mutual funds and a few individual stocks—he's not sure he understands. BT says he's just about out of time. Jim quickly asks where he can get more information? Will he get statements? And from whom? BT says Big-Time Portfolios sends quarterly statements. How is he structured? Big Time explains he manages a "hedge fund"—which means he doesn't have to register with the SEC, and isn't. But this is better for his clients. If he registered, he would have to divulge his proprietary strategy, and good-bye market advantage.

But BT encourages Jim to ask his golf partner, boss, and church buddies. They've been happy and can tell Jim all about it. But BT warns Jim—he prefers Jim doesn't talk to non-investors about the fund. Big Time wants to protect the exclusivity of his clients—he only lets "certain" people invest with him. Jim's friends really shouldn't have told him about Big Time, but Mr. B's OK this one time because he knows Jim's friends.

Jim can't quite believe that he's really going to be "in the club." Who does he make the check out to? Mr. Big says to Big Time LLC. Mr. B will personally deposit it. Jim hands Mr. B a check, they shake hands, and Jim walks out feeling like a million bucks—sure to get 15 percent a year forever.

How many red flags did you spot? The biggest was early on. Maybe Mr. Big Time is honorable and won't embezzle. But if he is a fraudster, or evolves into one, it's now simple to swindle Jim. Why? Jim failed to see the five signs of financial fraud. That's what this book is all about: Five simple signs that, if heeded, can help protect you from investing embezzlement.

## Don't Let Your Money Get "Madoff" With

2008 was miserable enough for most investors without finishing on news of Bernard Madoff bilking clients out of approximately $65 billion over 20 years. His victims included big names from all walks of life—from politics to Hollywood luminaries. But they weren't just big-pocketed stars. He reportedly bankrupted Holocaust survivor Elie Wiesel *and* his Foundation for Humanity. Madoff stole from many in his Jewish community, not all so wealthy either. Madoff accepted investors, big and small—an equal opportunity embezzler—fooling them with claims of exclusivity and consistently positive returns.

I needn't retread this—you've read about Madoff. Years from now folks will recall Madoff as the guy who used his powerful community connections to garner a big chunk of his victim's assets—which he then embezzled in a massive pyramid scheme. Turns out, many scamsters do this—prey on affinity groups. (This book details why they do and shows you how to spot it up front.)

And it wasn't just Madoff—2009 opened on endless news of similar scams, including the bizarre case of *Forbes* 400 member and Antiguan knight, Sir R. Allen Stanford. We'll cameo some of the most egregious cases—recent and historic. But a Google search renders more than you need.

This book doesn't aim to detail their deceptions, follow the money, or give you all their dirty laundry. There will be many books doing post mortems—and even more on the next round of big-time fraudsters. And there will be more future scams—100 percent certainty. Always are! No matter what regulators may devise, there will always be scamsters. We've had them since long before Charles Ponzi became synonymous with the timeless "rob Peter to pay Paul" swindle in 1920. The only thing to do is protect yourself.

So how can you ensure you never fall victim to the next Bernard Madoff, Stanford, or Ponzi?

# Just One Thing

In my 37 years managing money for individuals and institutions, 25 years writing the "Portfolio Strategy" column in *Forbes*, and a life-time studying markets, I've witnessed money managers—all kinds, good and bad. I've also seen and studied the occasional fraudster (and in truth, though sensational, they're very rare) who forgoes money management for thievery.

The thieves can be creative, but structurally the scams are similar. That's good news because avoiding a would-be con artist is easy, no matter how convincing he is. There are just a couple questions—one or two *tops*—you must ask to avoid most all scams. Be vigilant for a few more red flags, and you can have even better success. But, interestingly, most people don't know the questions to ask.

And because these rats are so despicable, I'll tell you—right here, right now—the number one most crucial thing you must do. I don't care if you're reading this in your favorite bookstore and never read another word. If I can help even one person not fall victim to a financial scam, I'll consider the time it took to write this book worth it.

You can avoid hiring a would-be thief by:

**Never hiring any form of money manager or adviser who takes custody of your assets.**

What does that mean? Said another way: Always make sure the decision maker (who will decide what you should own, like stocks, bonds, mutual funds, etc.) has no access to the money—meaning they can't get their hands on it directly. I'll explain what that means in more detail in Chapter 1. But, simply said, when you hire a money manager, you yourself should deposit the money with a third-party, reputable, sizable, big-name custodian wholly unconnected to the money manager or decision maker. That custodian's job is to safeguard the security of your assets. Do that—even if you do nothing else from this book—and you can mostly protect your money from being "Madoff" with.

If your adviser has access to the money because he controls or is somehow affiliated with whoever has custody of your assets, there is always, *always* the risk he carries your money out the back door. Maybe he's pure of heart and won't, but why risk it? Don't give him a chance.

## Better Yet, Here are Five Signs

Here are five signs your adviser might now be or could evolve into a swindling rat:

1. Your adviser also has custody of your assets—*the number one, biggest, reddest flag.*
2. Returns are consistently great! Almost *too good to be true.*
3. The investing strategy isn't understandable, is murky, flashy, or "too complicated" for him (her, or it) to describe so you easily understand.
4. Your adviser promotes benefits like exclusivity, which don't impact results.
5. You didn't do your own due diligence, but a trusted intermediary did.

This book examines each sign in detail—from a variety of perspectives—and shows you how to use them together like a checklist to help ensure a con never swindles you. Note: Just because your manager displays one or a few signs, it doesn't mean they should immediately be clapped in irons. Rather, these are signs your adviser may have the *means* to embezzle and a possible framework to deceive. Always better to be suspicious and safe than trusting and sorry. Remember, Madoff and Stanford (allegedly) ran their scams for years—Madoff for possibly two decades! Folks looked into their eyes and trusted them.

# Big or Small—a Con Wants 'em All

Madoff stole billions. Stanford's alleged to have done the same. Even some relatively "smaller" cons stole many millions. That may make smaller investors think they're safe. If you don't have a big bundle, a con artist won't be interested, right?

Dead wrong. The scandals you read about are sensational size-wise, but these scams go on endlessly on smaller scales in small towns everywhere. These don't make the papers—maybe not outside their regions—because the scams get outed before getting too big. But victims don't care if it was a big scam or small—they still lost everything. And even the biggest scams started small, once.

And successful con artists rely on their communities to supply victims (detailed in Chapter 4). Many intentionally prey on friends and neighbors—which means the small-town angle suits them fine. Madoff was based in Manhattan. But plenty of cons focus on smaller communities where their connections buy them less scrutiny—like Darren Palmer who terrorized Idaho Falls, Idaho, or Nicholas Cosmo, who based himself in Hauppauge, New York—a hamlet in Long Island a ways outside slick Manhattan.

## Small Fish, Big Rats

But smaller investors needn't fear con artists, right? Why would a con artist bother with them? Because they're rats. Big or small—they want them all. If you have money to invest—whether $10,000 or $10 million—some con wants you. They need constant incoming funds to support the pyramid—wherever they can get them. And as the scam wears on and they get desperate, they may increasingly turn to smaller investors—any investors—to keep money flowing in. And that's when you can get really hurt. They have no hesitation at all to take all your money and leave you penniless, knowing full well what they're doing and how it will impact you. There is no sympathy there. No soul. No guilt or remorse. It is a form of intentional activity that is no different from simple stealing—just gone about differently so they can get much more money from you than they could steal at gun point.

Also, don't be fooled by claims of exclusivity! First, this is a red flag. Second, it's a lie. Madoff claimed to be very exclusive. And you know from media reports he had big clients—hedge funds, billionaires, banks. *But he also accepted tiny, not-so-exclusive-at-all investors*—including retired school teachers.[1] Nothing wrong with school teachers, but they typically don't have billions. Some victims reported losing their life savings—of $100,000. Some victims had still less.[2]

Madoff, though a long-time successful rat, is no different from any other con artist rat. They *project* exclusivity intentionally, hoping you'll feel grateful they're letting you into their club. They want victims to *think* they're safe so they won't be fearful and suspicious as the scam is put in place and continued. They want victims to think that an adviser for really big investors can't be a con artist—those big investors are smart. Wrong way to think! Cons have ways of netting big fish, but they want little fish, too—and more of them. Little fish, medium fish, big fish—they can all get conned. As long as you don't think the rat himself smells fishy, *you* can get conned. (But no more, because you'll follow this book's prescriptions and avoid getting embezzled.)

In fact, smaller investors *should* be disproportionately worried. These kinds of financial frauds typically create a façade mimicking a discretionary adviser. Many discretionary advisers, particularly larger, legit ones, have firm minimums—discussed more in Chapter 4. Maybe that's $100,000, $1 million, or vastly more. They set some level under which they feel they're too inefficient to help clients much. That's fine and normal. Why charge you fees if you won't get much benefit?

What's *not* normal is for some swaggering, supposed big-time adviser with big-time clients to claim to have high minimums, but just this once, just for you, he'll gladly take you, Mr. Little-For-Now, with your ten grand. This is just the opposite of what a legit adviser will do. If a legit adviser has account minimums, they stick to them pretty strictly. If you meet an adviser who talks like Mr. Big Shot and is anxious to invest your $5,000 IRA contribution, be very, very worried. Some clever cons will specifically cast for small fish—because they know they won't have a long investing history to compare them to.

Big or small—$10,000 to invest or $100 million—all five of this book's rules apply.

### Fool Me Once

Folks may think, "Those people were fooled. But I wouldn't be fooled. I'm very smart." Probably very true! Just remember: Victims were fooled, but they weren't stupid. People who aren't fools are often fooled. Of Madoff's alleged $65 billion swindle, $36 billion came from just 25 investors—including hedge funds, charities, and even some super big, rich, influential and sophisticated individuals. You don't become a $1 billion-plus investor by being stupid or a fool. Perhaps they weren't suspicious enough, but not overt fools. They were smart and they were fooled. A dose of cynicism can help protect you from becoming so victimized.

## Bear Markets Don't Cause Scams

Were 2008 and 2009 so unusual in having so many scams? Hardly! Bear markets reveal scams, but bear markets don't *cause* scams. Madoff did it for decades—2008 just popped him out into the open when he couldn't keep it going any longer, as bear markets and recessions do for many scamster rats. If a scamster successfully avoids detection long enough to get enough money from victims, big volatility simply unmasks deceptions—for a few reasons. First, downturns make it harder to bring in new money. A pyramid scam needs constant new money to cover distributions to older investors. Without fresh money, it collapses.

Also, investors in general, even in perfectly legit investment vehicles, tend to get fearful and redeem shares during downturns, putting additional pressure on fraudsters. Or perhaps one or two investors get curious as to why they're getting positive returns when everyone else is down—though this introspection is actually very rare and con artists rely on that. Scamster rats tend to be pretty charismatic with pretty, fancy whiskers, claws, and tales instead of tails—but enough frank scrutiny from victims can be their undoing.

This is why, in a bear's depths, scams get uncovered. Media and politicians label these "indictments of the era," saying the "excesses" of previous good times and some lack of oversight created the fraud. (Pretty much every market and/or economic downturn is blamed on excesses of the previous period—always been that way since the Tulip Bubble in 1637, and probably before.) Wrong! The fraudster created the fraud—no one and nothing else—and market volatility uncovered it. A fraudster is never an indictment of any era—he's just an indictment of his own soulless black heart. He's a rat. We've always had human rats. These are bad criminals and must be thought of as solely criminals—to be put in a rat cage and not let out. They are stylistically different, but otherwise no different from criminals that engage in larceny, burglary, and theft. No one would say the detection of a house burglar is an "indictment of an era"—so these guys' detection isn't an indictment of anything but themselves.

## Normal Market Volatility Is Just that—Normal

During periods of big volatility, some may feel they've been cheated. A thief steals your money, and the market dings your portfolio—sometimes hard. Is there really a difference?

Absolutely! Market volatility is normal—thievery is not, as shown in Chapter 2. Perfectly good and healthy firms like Procter & Gamble or Coca-Cola experience wild stock price swings—in good economic times and bad. And the broad market periodically goes through stomach-churning corrections and soul-crushing bear markets. Yet after bear markets are over, stocks come back—and the stocks that got cut in half, for example, can come back faster than you might have feared, making you whole again. Over long periods, stocks have averaged about 10 percent a year (see Table 2.1), depending on how and when you measure—and that *includes* big down times. But the money a con takes from you never, ever comes back. Gone forever!

Over the long term, equities are likeliest to give you better returns relative to cash or bonds[3]—but it's never a smooth ride. Bull markets feel wonderful and bear markets nauseating. But over time, stocks have been a great long-term investment vehicle for investors who have had the stomach to ride it out.

Ironically, this is exactly opposite to what Madoff, Stanford, and hundreds of other scamming villains have claimed over the years. Many of their victims were fooled by claims of consistently positive, high, but largely stable and non-volatile returns. The problem: Those big, smooth, positive returns Madoff's and Stanford's investors thought they got were carefully constructed fiction. It's hard to escape this universal investing fact: If you want market-like returns, you must accept market-like volatility. No way around that. Anyone telling you otherwise may have malevolent intent.

Bear markets are followed by bulls eventually, forever and ever, Amen. Always been that way, and unless aliens invade or the body snatchers win, I'll bet it will keep being that way. As much as things change, things stay the same—particularly people. Which is why, no matter how much effort regulators and politicians put into protecting we the people from villains, someone will always be scamming, and some will do so spectacularly. But starting now, you don't need to fear you might be hiring a Madoff-redux. Read this book, follow its five simple rules, and you can avoid suffering an investing embezzlement or Ponzi scheme of any form. Rat free!

This is my sixth book, including two *New York Times* bestsellers. After Madoff, I feel like it should have been my first book. And if an investor asked me which of my books I thought he or she should read first, it would be this one—because sometimes the return *of* your money is simply a lot more important than the return *on* your money. And that's what this book is all about—making sure you can always have the return of your money. I hope you like it.

# Chapter 1

# Good Fences
# Make Good Neighbors

Fortunately for our friend Jim from the Introduction, the SEC and FBI shut down Big-Time Portfolios almost immediately after his meeting—before his check was even cashed. Now Jim must find someone else to manage his money. He wants someone trustworthy—he was beyond lucky to escape unscathed last time. He won't be fooled again.

A few towns over, he finds Trusty Time LLC. They manage a few billion and have been around a while—so they must be safe. And they're big enough that they do money management and are their own broker-dealer, so Jim can write them a check and deposit his money directly with them. Jim thinks that's convenient! Cuts down on his paperwork.

Jim's headed straight for trouble again. He's considering a decision maker who takes custody of assets—financial fraud sign number one.

# Sign #1    Your Adviser Also Has Custody of Your Assets.

In December 2008, a long-standing, well-regarded member of the finance community, former NASDAQ chairman and member of SEC advisory committees, huge charitable contributor, and New York and Palm Beach society pillar admitted to his sons the $65 billion he managed for hedge funds, charities, foundations, Hollywood stars, and Jewish grandmothers was a fraud. A pyramid scheme. The money—gone. Lots of fortunes blown—and minds blown.

Then oddly came Texas-born Antiguan knight "Sir" R. Allen Stanford. A repeat *Forbes* 400 member, the SEC charged that the $8 billion he managed was a Ponzi scheme. As 2009 began more scams surfaced. Indiana hedge fund manager Marcus Schrenker faked his own death—staged a plane crash—to escape authorities closing in on his alleged scam.[1] New Yorker Nicholas Cosmo was charged with making fake bridge loans and swindling $370 million.[2] Philly man Joseph S. Forte was charged with running a $50 million Ponzi.[3]

As more details emerged about all these swindles, folks wanted to know what happened. Who did what and how? How did they avoid detection? Will they be punished? Where did the money go, and will victims get any back? Good questions, but the most important and this book's purpose:

How can I make sure it never, ever happens to me?

An age-old Western saying related to how to keep people from stealing things from your wide open spaces is "good fences make good neighbors." To avoid being victimized by a future Madoff-style Ponzi scheme (because there will be more—count on it), that's the single best advice. I'm going to show you how to easily build a great fence against financial embezzlement of any form. It's the single most important thing you can do. I've studied the recent cases and history's biggest cases, and they all have one thing in common—financial fraud sign number one: *The money manager also had custody of the assets.*

In other words, the money manager or financial adviser also acts as the bank or broker/dealer—holding and supposedly safekeeping the assets he/she/it manages. Clients didn't deposit the money with a third party—they deposited the money directly with the decision maker. Then, it's the decision maker's responsibility not only to decide to buy this stock and not that one, but also to keep and account for the money and all securities that may be owned.

In taking custody, the adviser entity literally has the ability to spend the money in any way it sees fit or take it out the back door and flee to Mexico—any old time he wants. Some set their businesses up this way intentionally to embezzle. Others start honest but later fall to the temptation to exaggerate returns. In my view, the latter happens more often than the former but it's just as devastating to you if it happens. It doesn't matter that your adviser started out with good intent, only that you got embezzled.

Separating the two functions—custody and decision making—is prophylactic. The very, very few instances historically where the money manager didn't have direct access through custody and still embezzled, he could somehow manipulate the custodian (one example I'll describe later). Identify those cases, figure out how to avoid them (using this book's other chapters), and then your success in preventing your money from being Madoff with should be just about 100 percent perfect.

If the manager has custody, he can take money out the back door—any time he wants. Don't give any adviser that opportunity, no matter what. They may start completely honestly, but if they fall to temptation later like Madoff did, you're not protected at all—completely vulnerable.

That doesn't mean there aren't valid reasons to combine custody with decision making at the same firm. There are. But you must confirm a rock-solid, nuclear-proof firewall exists between the two functions. Otherwise, it's simply a disaster waiting to happen.

# A Ponzi by Any Other Name

Just because Madoff is safely behind bars, don't assume the world's now safe from his brand of disaster. Though he and Stanford were big news in 2009, this kind of scam is nothing new. History is littered with rats, big and small, who helped themselves to client money—whether the clients had millions or a few thousand. Madoff made headlines because of the scale and scope of his long con, but what he allegedly did—a Ponzi scheme—has been around since long before Charles Ponzi gave this con a name in 1920.

And there will—100 percent certainty—be more future cons; always have, always will. You must remain vigilant to protect yourself. Try as regulators and politicians might, there will always be black-hearted thieves and enough folks to victimize who believe big returns without risk are possible. (More on too-good-to-be-true returns in Chapter 2.) And inflation surely means future cons will be bigger dollar-wise. But no matter the size, they almost all had (and likely will have) the same feature: The rats are decision makers who also have custody of client assets.

## Same Scam, Different Scamsters

And just who are these rats? Were it not for the Madoff scandal being uncovered just weeks before, "Sir" Stanford's $8 billion (alleged) swindle would have been history's all-time biggest scam. He almost set the record, but he simply paled in comparison to Madoff. It will be some time, I suspect, before someone out-Madoffs Madoff and makes off with a new all-time record rat attack.

But before them was the infamous 1970s fugitive Robert Vesco. In 1970, this charismatic con artist "rescued" a troubled $400 million

## When the Pyramid Became a Ponzi

Why did Ponzi become synonymous with robbing Peter to pay Paul? Though uneducated with a background as a laborer, clerk, fruit peddler, waiter, and smuggler, Ponzi was also handsome, slim, dapper, self-assured, and quick witted—which let him look and sound the part once he shifted to finance.

In 1920, he placed a simple newspaper ad, promising a 50 percent return in just 45 days—or *100* percent in 90—playing currency spreads by trading International Postage Union reply coupons. The money flowed in—which was good for him—because he wasn't investing it. He used new investor money to pay older investors. But it worked! For a while—until the *Boston Post* investigated. Turns out only $75,000 in reply coupons were normally printed in a given year—but six months into his scam, Ponzi had taken in millions! He couldn't possibly have invested it all.

Ponzi responded by offering *doubled* interest payments. You'd think folks would be scared off, but instead money kept flooding in. Finally, the *Boston Post*—not regulators, mind you—revealed Ponzi's firm as virtually penniless. Ponzi had taken in about $10 million, issued notes for $14 million, but his accounts held less than $200,000. Ponzi didn't spend all $10 million, though undoubtedly he spent some. It appeared most went to pay his earliest investors—like any pyramid. This is the very basis of what is now famously called a Ponzi scheme.

His pyramid-based cash flow let him actually buy controlling interest in Hanover Trust Company, where he brazenly made himself president shortly before his scheme was blown apart. Crowds adored him, followed him, chanted to him—until the gig was up. He had a mansion and servants. For a very brief period, he had a charmed life, high on the hog.

But he was clearly a con man from the get-go. You could see from his prior history as a smuggler that he wasn't integrity-constrained. Later, while out on bail pending appeal, he sold underwater swamp lots in Florida, making another small fortune before going to the big house for 12 years. Italian born, when he was released from prison he was immediately deported to Italy and then moved to Rio de Janeiro, where he lived a meager life until his death in 1949 in a Rio charity hospital. At death he had $75.

Source: Matthew Josephson, *The Money Lords*, Weybright and Talley, Inc., 1972, pp. 35–36; Robert Sobel, *The Great Bull Market*, W.W. Norton & Co., Inc., 1968, pp.17–20, 98.

mutual fund from its previous owner—who himself ran afoul of the SEC. Investors hoped Vesco would improve returns. Instead, Vesco carted off $224 million. He then bounced from the Bahamas to Costa Rica to finally Cuba, reportedly keeping his money in numbered Swiss bank accounts and dribbling payments over time to Fidel Castro in exchange for protection from Western world authorities. While I'm sure this was lucrative for Castro, he probably also enjoyed housing Vesco—it created a thorn in the side of the US Department of Justice, who saw Vesco as a top-10 wanted criminal for a very long time. Never brought to justice, Vesco apparently died in Cuba, though many believe he faked his own death—another routine escape-artist act.[4]

But Vesco's wasn't even the biggest swindle up to that time! That distinction for many years went to Ivar Kreuger—the Match King—who swindled $250 million before his pyramid toppled in 1932. Kreuger ran an audacious scam—offering shockingly cheap loans to sovereign nations in return for monopoly distribution of his safety matches. He kept capital flowing in by offering ridiculously high dividends to investors and escaped detection by cooking the books and bribing countries with ever-lower rates. He bamboozled investors with flashy displays and a slick appearance. He, too, lived high. Fancy suits, countless mistresses—at least a dozen documented at one time in different European cities, all on allowance and decked in diamonds and silk—and this after the 1929 crash! (I'm always amazed Kreuger isn't better known now—he was such a huge, famous villain. A bio of him from my 1993 book, *100 Minds That Made the Market*, is excerpted in Appendix C.)

Like all Ponzis, it couldn't last—distributions overwhelmed incoming funds, which is the normal undoing of most Ponzi schemes. In March 1932, he had a nervous breakdown, couldn't sleep, and answered imaginary phone calls and door knocks. Eventually, dressed to the nines, he lay on a bed, unbuttoned his pin-striped suit and silk monogrammed shirt, and hand-gunned himself.[5]

## An Unending Rat Pack

History's rat parade is effectively endless. Market volatility in 2008 and 2009 uncovered a whole new rat pack.

- Nicholas Cosmo—the $370 million rat—promised *80 percent returns* by providing private bridge loans to commercial real estate firms. It doesn't appear many—if any—such loans were made.[6]
- Arthur Nadel, a one-time lawyer previously disbarred for investing escrow funds, was charged with a $350 million hedge fund scam. He claimed *12 percent monthly returns* in 2008—actual fund returns were negative. What the market didn't take, he allegedly did. The FBI is still investigating.[7]
- Daren Palmer ran a textbook Ponzi (allegedly, still being investigated) in Idaho Falls. He's charged with swindling $100 million— boasting *40 percent annual returns*. He gave himself a $35,000 salary, a $12 million home, a fleet of snowmobiles, and likely a one-way ticket to federal prison.[8]
- Robert Brown from Hillsborough, California—the town next to where I was raised—was charged with scamming $20 million by promising to double investments in 13 months. He also promised if clients lost money, he'd cover the difference—out of his own pocket![9] He didn't take care of clients. He just took them to the cleaners.

And the theme repeats through history.

- Kirk Wright rocked the NFL—ripping off former and current pros with a $185 million hedge fund scam that crumbled in 2006.[10]

- In 2008, the SEC convicted Alberto Vilar with stealing $5 million from hedge fund investors for personal use and giving away much more to opera houses globally. A fondness for fine arts does not necessarily translate to honesty and good sense.[11]
- After being banned for life by the SEC in 1991 for securities crimes, Martin Frankel was undaunted. He bought small, troubled insurance firms, pillaged their reserves, plundered premiums, and dummied financials to make them look healthier—using them to lever purchases of more firms to rob. Meanwhile, he contacted the Vatican to set up a fake charity—to scam still more! In 1999, he was charged with defrauding investors of $208 million— then he absconded to Germany. He was later brought to justice, serving time both in Germany and America.[12] A globe-trotting rat.
- David Dominelli, outed in 1984, served 20 years in prison for his scam. He swindled about $80 million through his currency trading firm, J. David Company.[13] His victims were largely San Diego's wealthy. He so ingratiated himself, he took down San Diego's then-mayor, Roger Hedgecock, who was charged with taking illegal contributions from the con artist and forced from office.
- Richard Whitney, *president of the New York Stock Exchange* (a lot like Madoff) in the 1930s, ripped off $2 million or more—a princely sum during the Great Depression. Never take an impressive resume at face value.

Just a few examples. And before them all is an unending line of black-hearted thieves and pirates. Rats! They had different ploys to lure marks. Struck different victims—large and small. Some were global; some preferred terrorizing their own small towns. But they all—*all*—had one major thing in common: **They all had access to the till.** They made sure of that. A rat has to have access to the cheese. Take away the access, and they probably do no more damage than a Three-Card Monte street hustler. And if you don't give them that access—refuse to hand over decision making—then you are safe.

## What Victims Look Like

Or are you? This book teaches how to spot the rats, but what do victims look like? Like *you*? Maybe! You already know victims come from all walks—with billions or pennies. But what makes someone more likely to be conned?

In my 37-year career managing money, 25 years writing the *Forbes* "Portfolio Strategy" column, writing five other books, and generally touring and speaking with investors—hundreds of speeches—I've interacted with lots of investors—many, many thousands. My firm itself has more than 20,000 clients. Having studied them, profiled them, watched countless focus groups of them, and surveyed them, I consider investors of all sizes and types fit pretty darned tightly into one of six categories. They can all be victims of embezzlement. But understanding who these investor types are and how they generally think helps you see what you have to do to stay safe. You're likely one of the following:

- **Confident Clark**. Professional help? Pah! You're just as good as any of them. No—better! Plus, you enjoy everything about investing. You're a do-it-yourselfer—no one but you is going to make decisions on your money. You love getting reports and stock tips and charting your own course.
- **Hobby Hal**. Investing is a serious pursuit—like a full-time job. You like educating yourself and being active in portfolio decisions and "talking shop." You might use an adviser, but it's definitely a two-way business partnership, with you making the final call. It's your very serious hobby.
- **Expert Ellen**. You enjoy studying and learning about markets—it's fun! You check in regularly on how your investments are doing, but admittedly you're often too busy to keep up as much as you'd like. You like having a professional partner and may even have them make your investment decisions—you appreciate the value a good professional provides. Besides, you really don't have the time to do it yourself—too busy being Chief Executive Something.

- **Daunted Dave**. You don't feel comfortable making investing decisions without professional help. Investing is complex and intimidating—it's not fun, plus you don't have time nor want to make time. You don't read or watch much financial media. Having a professional make decisions for you gives you peace of mind, so you can focus on the parts of life you really enjoy and consider yourself good at.
- **Concerned Carl**. You worry you won't meet your investing goals and don't feel confident making important decisions for yourself. You don't have time to adequately manage your money—you want a professional handling decisions for you. You'll probably ask lots of questions, but to be honest, you aren't entirely sure what to do with the answers.
- **Avoidance Al**. You don't want to deal with investing, ever! (Heck, you're probably not reading this book.) You don't like thinking about it, doing it, or even thinking about hiring someone to do it for you. It's all too overwhelming, and in some ways feels inappropriate to be talked about—maybe a little like sex, it's certainly not dinner conversation. You'll think about it next week (month, year, decade).

We know Clark isn't hiring a con artist—he isn't hiring anyone! Hal might hire an adviser, but a con artist probably doesn't want him either. Hal's way too involved for a con artist to feel comfortable that Hal won't get into the middle of things. Ellen will be less constantly involved—which a con prefers—but she'll likely not be conned by big returns (Chapter 2), and she'll question too hard. Not optimal for fraudsters.

Dave could definitely run into trouble. Dave doesn't have the time or the inclination to learn more than he has to. Worse, Dave probably doesn't do much due diligence. He'll take referrals gladly from his tennis buddy, his neighbor, his dog walker. Dave's too busy to dig—he wants to be told what to do by someone he thinks he can trust, and he'll do it.

I worry about Carl, because Carl is a worrier. He frets he can't hit investing goals without a professional. No way he can do it! He wants

## Daunted Dave in Hollywood

The media was amazed that big-name Hollywood stars fell for Madoff. I'm not. Believe it or not, they're daunted, like Dave. So too were Kirk Wright's sports stars. Classic daunted investors. They don't have time. Plus, big-time stars and athletes can be very isolated. Movie stars in particular are sheltered from the real world and most of their financial decisions are made by their managers. They feel isolated and unable to deal with the real world because the real world makes such a fuss over them. Often, they're simply not safe in public. They get very few real-world interactions of the type you take for granted every day. They're daunted and they trust their managers implicitly, which is why they've delegated so many functions to them—including picking asset managers. So, the daunted may rely even more heavily on referrals—which con artists really love (discussed more in Chapter 4).

to hand decision-making over entirely—goes looking for help. Con artists like to be looked for. Con artists also love Carl because complex mumbo-jumbo nonsense (Chapter 3) works on him. (E.g., "We look for beta volumetric opportunities in mid-cap value Pan-Asian tech stocks, and hedge to take full advantage with minimal risk using complex derivatives and mythorian algorithms.") Carl thinks that sounds smart, and that works just great for rats.

Now, Al may avoid hiring a con artist, just because he avoids doing anything at all! But once he decides to hire someone, he never checks back, and likely doesn't find out he's been conned until after the media fanfare, after the trial, and after the villain's been cooling his heels in jail for six years.

Con artists love Dave, Carl, even Al. If you see yourself in one of them, you're more likely to hire a pro, but you're also more likely to be conned. But don't make the mistake of thinking, "I'm like Clark! I'll never be taken in. I never need to worry." This is like being told by your doctor you have a low risk of heart disease, so you don't take care of your health.

You may feel like Clark or Ellen right now. But the same investor can actually morph over time into someone else—happens all the time. The way investors see their needs can easily change. During bull markets, investors are more likely to say they want growth and aren't risk averse. They're not conservative, no! They want zooming stocks. They're confident and tough. Maybe they don't need professional help at all! They want to pick their own investments. Then, they may feel more like Clark, Ellen, or Hal—eager to engage, feeling confident.

But after a bear market knocks their stocks down, those same, confident, tough-guy (or gal) investors may change. Not only do they now want capital preservation, but they often believe that's all they ever wanted! Growth? Who ever wanted growth? Not them! Same investor—and they'll swear they haven't changed. Their long-term goals certainly haven't. But what they say they want has. The bull market made them confident, but the bear market made them daunted. And that's when a con artist strikes.

## The Big Swindle

So how can you rat out the rat? By knowing how they operate. No matter what the window dressing, no matter the psychological ploys, the rat's fundamental operation is the same. They sell themselves as chief decision maker. Then they have clients deposit assets in a custodial institution they control or in an account they control—allowing them to plunder at will. An intended con man will set up this way with the intent to embezzle. Others just fall into it. Either way, doesn't matter. Structurally, the possibility exists if there's no division between decision maker and custodian. They can inflate asset values and issue false statements. They can shift money or drain it entirely. Who will stop them? They're in charge of the piggy bank—no one else.

Why would an honest person set up a financial advice or money management firm this way? Because it's simply easier for the operator. How does a seemingly honest person evolve into a swindler? Usually, in my view, they have a personal problem that requires temporary money,

## Don't Take Anything for Granted

An important lesson: First, Ponzis are nothing new. Second: Anyone can fall victim.

Former US President Ulysses S. Grant was himself victimized by a pyramid scheme—years before Ponzi thought about hawking postage stamps. Grant was perhaps equally as famous for his battlefield heroics as he was for his financial failings. He was financially made and undone a number of times—falling for a scheme to corner the gold market that failed and getting involved in risky Nevada mining operations.

But his final undoing was a classic pyramid. Grant lent his name to a family friend, Ferdinand Ward, in opening a brokerage business—Grant and Ward. Grant wasn't involved in operations, just a figurehead. His name gave the business respectability—Civil War veterans by the hundreds invested with them.

Unfortunately, Ward not only didn't invest well, he didn't invest at all. He paid out dividends from incoming money. He finally admitted to Grant they were in financial trouble, and Grant, believing in Ward, asked for a $150,000 loan from railroad king and friend William Vanderbilt. Vanderbilt gladly lent the money, but soon that too was gone. And then Ward disappeared.

Grant tried to pay off the loan to Vanderbilt by giving him his home, his horse farm, and all his belongings. Vanderbilt refused to accept. Grant was already destitute; Vanderbilt didn't want him homeless too. Grant spent his final days writing his memoirs to try to earn a little something for his wife to live on.

If a US President can fall prey to a Ponzi, who can't? You can—don't give Ward or anyone else access to your assets.

Source: Lynn Fabian Lasner, "The Rise and Fall of Ulyssess S. Grant," *Humanities*, January/February 2002, 23(1).

and they simultaneously have what they see as a sure-fire investment opportunity. In their mind they're going to "borrow" the money for a while, make the investment in their own name, get a big one-time return, put back the "borrowed" money, and then pocket the profits to cover their personal problem.

Of course, the surefire investment opportunity blows up and they can't return the "borrowed" money. So they falsify statements, use new investors to cover losses for older investors, and borrow more to bet again on another surefire investment opportunity they think will bail them out—and it doesn't either. It goes down too. Soon they give up on anything else but recruiting new investor money to cover older investors, and hope they can keep doing that—which they only can by faking financial statements, claiming very high but very stable and desirable returns, and selling hard.

If there's no division between decision maker and custodian, a rat can inflate asset values, issue false statements, shift money around, or steal it entirely. They're in charge of the piggy bank.

During his arraignment, Madoff claimed he didn't begin misapplying client funds until the early 1990s—in response to a rocky year—in what he hoped would be a short-lived solution that snowballed.[14] It's no excuse, but had he set himself up without access, he simply couldn't have fallen to temptation. He would have had to admit to losses, as many thousands of honest money managers and financial advisers routinely do every year. The very best long-term money managers have had some rocky years. But some folks don't have the stuff to own up to mistakes, learn from them, and move on. Some would rather cover them, maybe fudging the numbers and doubling down to make it up, believing no one will be the wiser. Madoff didn't have the stuff.

It's not just illegal and amoral—it's fundamentally backward. More risk from doubling down can mean bigger potential future losses. When doubled-down bets go awry, you're really in a hole. All the while, the manager is reporting good returns, using incoming assets to cover the tracks of his losses. Eventually, the thing blows up—always.

I have no way of knowing how many fraudsters started fine but later evolved to sliminess, but it doesn't matter. By simply setting it up so they don't have access to client funds, they can't manipulate your returns and misapply your funds.

## When the Fox Owns the Henhouse

How did Madoff do it? Madoff's advisory clients deposited assets directly with Madoff Investment Securities. Madoff Securities, on its own, appeared to be a legit, long-standing firm. Founded in 1960, at its height it handled $1 trillion in trades per year, making it one of the top-three market makers in both NYSE and NASDAQ securities globally.[15] That's really pretty impressive. You wouldn't logically think someone who had gotten that far in life would devolve to crime.

But it wasn't the brokerage operation that was the problem for people. There's really nothing there to raise alarm—until the fellow with the name on the piggy bank became an asset manager, running an LLC that took custody of people's money and made investment decisions for them. Then it becomes tactically nothing for him to steal, if he chooses. And Madoff chose, claiming he didn't start out to swindle but fell into it. But he appears to have been an exceptional student of the game.

"Sir" Stanford did the same (allegedly—as of this writing). Though Madoff stole more, Stanford seems to me a particularly loathsome villain. Did he specifically set his business up intentionally to defraud? That's for courts to decide. But as a disinterested onlooker, I'm suspicious he did—he was the fox who owned the henhouse. He set up a bank—Stanford International Bank—based in Antigua. By all accounts, the bank does engage in some normal, non-criminal banking activity. But why Antigua? Because if I were a would-be villain, I'd want to choose a spot where I knew I could easily buy influence—hence better not in America—better in a small, poor place where you could more easily make a big impact on the government.

Note: This isn't to say Antigua was in cahoots. Rather, in a smaller, cash-strapped nation, it's likely easier to pay a regulator or two to wink at peccadilloes. That's why Robert Vesco ended up in Cuba. Further, Stanford was Antigua-Barbuda's second-largest employer, after the government.[16] If you've ever been there, you know it is a tiny little place, with most people living in abject poverty with a heavy dependence on cruise-based tourism. In a small, poor country, Stanford became the biggest fish in the pond. Did he know his hosts wouldn't eagerly question and look into the big employer, who built soccer and cricket stadiums and showered the island with charitable contributions?

Stanford's bank issued certificates of deposit (CDs) with ultra-high interest rates—much higher than you could get from a normal bank (a red flag covered in Chapter 2)—based on the bank's "unique" investment strategy. (Unfortunately, it may have been "unique" like the Tooth Fairy is unique.) The CDs were sold primarily through Stanford's advisory business, Stanford Capital Management, and assets were held at his broker-dealer, Stanford Group Company.

At every turn, Stanford had access. (Vital rule: If it looks suspicious in terms of custody, it is suspicious and should be avoided!) Making matters worse, his businesses were operated by family and friends—a close inner circle—including his father and college roommate. Perhaps Stanford's top executives didn't intend to be fraudsters—again, up to the courts—but it appears he arranged matters, giving him maximum access with minimal outside objection. In fact, the court-appointed receiver, charged with overseeing Stanford's businesses while the SEC continues its investigation, said, "The structure was seemingly designed to obfuscate holdings and transfers of cash and assets."[17](Stanford's response was that the receiver is a "jerk.")[18]

Such an arrangement is the ultimate red flag. Clients believed they were buying safe bank CDs. The outrageous interest rates, much higher than other banks, should have raised alarm. But the biggest mistake was buying a Stanford CD from a Stanford salesperson deposited in a Stanford custodial institution. Insisting on separation would have saved you from victimhood.

## Commingling Cons

Some scamsters lack the prestige, resources, or both to set up a custodial institution. Not everyone can start a broker-dealer or a bank—takes time, money, or partners with big pockets (an additional scam layer that's harder to pull off). But this doesn't preclude anyone from thieving. Instead, they can open a brokerage account or series of accounts—wholly under their control—and commingle client assets. Then, it's easy to withdraw at will—there's no clear delineation between what's yours, what's someone else's, and what the fraudster takes.

When you allow your money to be commingled, there's no clear delineation between what's yours, what's someone else's, and what the rat wants to steal. Insist on a separate account in your name at a third-party custodian.

This is easier for small-time scamsters—anyone can open a brokerage account—though perhaps a bit harder to convince folks you're a legit operation. But this is how many hedge funds operate! They commingle assets in a single or several accounts. Amazingly, something as simple as an Ameritrade account can be used to swindle millions. This is just what Kirk Wright did. He ran a $185 million hedge fund fraud lasting from 1996 to 2006—all through a few plain-vanilla Ameritrade accounts.[19](He has since been convicted of, among other things, securities fraud and money laundering. And, in another dramatic turn, similar to the Match King, he hung himself in his cell in 2008.)[20]

There's nothing wrong with Ameritrade—not at all. Perfectly fine place to custody assets. The problem was Kirk Wright deposited client money in accounts he controlled. He had full access but clients had none. Even if they had gotten some form of access, because assets were commingled, they couldn't tell what was rightly theirs.

## What If the Firm Goes Bankrupt?

Another reason to park your assets at a big, major name, non-connected broker-dealer or bank? You are better protected in case the firm becomes insolvent.

Note that when Lehman failed in September 2008—failed completely!—those who had securities custodied there were fine. Yes, stocks were down, market like, but *clients still owned those securities in their portfolios.* They didn't go "poof" with Lehman. Clients simply moved securities to another custodian.

That's the beauty of owning securities in a separate account at a non-connected, major custodian—you just pick them up and deposit them elsewhere; no one can steal them. There is a complete and hard firewall between that custodial function and the rest of the firm—always. Those securities are yours, no matter what happens to the piggy bank where you've deposited them. And in the age of digital accounting, as opposed to moving physical stock certificates, it's even easier to transport your stocks should the broker-dealer fail, get wobbly, or simply not provide service you care for.

Whether it's major banks like Wells Fargo or JP Morgan Chase; major brokerages like Schwab, Fidelity, Merrill Lynch, Morgan Stanley, Smith Barney, UBS; or smaller but still substantial and publicly traded brokerage firms like Raymond James, at least the custody function leaves your assets whole and embezzle-proof.

## Master Manipulators

As stated before, you're almost entirely safe from embezzlers by depositing assets in a big, third-party custodian. There are exceptions—if the decision maker is in some form of collusion with or can otherwise manipulate the custodian, whether the custodian knows it or not. This has become beyond exceedingly tough to do in the Internet age—better for you—but it still isn't completely impossible. This is why you don't just want a third-party custodian—you want a big, deep-pocketed one who can make you whole in the event your decision maker goes rogue.

It happened not too long ago. Frank Gruttadauria (mentioned briefly in my 2008 book *The Ten Roads to Riches*) allegedly stole anywhere from $40 million to $115 million from 50 clients—but it's hard to know exactly how much. He inflated account values, so clients believed when it all blew up that they lost much more.

He was an SG Cowen stock broker, then a Lehman Brothers branch manager in Cleveland. Lehman's gone now, but at the time, both were big, nationally known outfits. Gruttadauria persuaded many clients to give him discretion—so he wasn't just a custodian in his normal function as a broker, he also became the decision maker. (Nowadays, broker-dealers are reluctant to allow in-house brokers to take full discretion, but it still happens—be on alert.)

Still, Lehman was a big outfit with layers of client security. However, as branch manager, Gruttadauria had enough power to manipulate. First, he had oversight of other employees, including the branch compliance officer. Talk about conflict of interest! How likely are you to cast dispersions on the guy who decides how big your bonus is?

Second, Gruttadauria set up post boxes in his clients' names and had the real statements Lehman issued sent there. With help from his assistant (so the SEC charges), he created fake statements on official-looking Lehman letterhead and mailed those to his clients. Meanwhile, Gruttadauria was generating big losses by actively trading. The active trading generated big commissions for him and his firm—which kept his firm happy. To cover his losses—from poor management and outright stealing—he overstated account values, which kept clients docile. Clients were all too happy to "let it ride," but if one requested a distribution, Gruttadauria wrote a check out of another account—classic Ponzi-style.[21]

After Gruttadauria was finally outed by a heads-up granny who wanted online access, Cowen and Lehman together settled with the SEC and the NYSE—paying $7.5 million in fees and restitution.[22] The silver lining: Because Lehman was a big-pocketed firm, they were on the hook for what Gruttadauria stole. Very ironically, the problem comes in identifying exactly how much he stole and from whom in his giant shell game. The lawsuits continue to this day.[23]

But how does finding out your portfolio was an inflated fiction for years make you feel? Imagine a hypothetical scenario: As a client, you deposit $100,000. Statements over 15 years show big growth—you think you have maybe $800,000. Then you discover it's all been one big lie. Big Name Brokerage agrees to cover your losses. But because your broker was a thief and a liar, you never actually had the $800,000 that you believed you had, nor was it even reasonable to expect based on what the strategy purportedly was, so your settlement is for much less! No one wins.

Gruttadauria's scheme is harder to pull off in the Internet age—you can easily check account balances online directly from the custodian. And make sure you do! But no doubt, someone somewhere will figure out a way, yet it's so easy to protect yourself.

## Building a Good Fence

How can you protect yourself? Insist on a good fence. If someone is making investment decisions for you, be sure he, she, or it is separate from whoever has custody of your money. That's it. Have your assets held at a major-name custodian—a major bank like Wells Fargo or Bank of America or a major brokerage firm like Schwab, Merrill Lynch, Fidelity, UBS, or the like. There are many, and all are fine and similar in terms of safety—you choose. Have someone else, non-connected, make decisions about what to buy and sell. End of embezzlement story.

No matter how big, how reputable the money manager is, if your assets are deposited in an institution—whether a bank, broker-dealer, or other depository institution—somehow connected to the decision maker, you run the risk he, she, or it will plunder. And if not the chief decision maker, then one of its employees.

### Bigger Is Better

Why does the custodian have to be big with a big name? Think it through another way. Joe and Moe set out to swindle you. Joe claims to be the investment guru. He takes you to Moe who runs Moe Money Custody

Inc. as a supposed independent third-party custodian. Joe tells you because Moe is independent, your money will be safe there. You give your money to Moe, then Moe and Joe go and take your money out the back door and off to Antigua, and you can't find them or your money ever again. It isn't sufficient just to have a separate custodian from your decision maker, but to have one you're sure your decision maker can't possibly collude with. The only way to do that with surety is have the custodian be big, big name, and completely independent so the decision maker can't possibly collude to swindle.

But also insist on an account with *your* name on it. Fine, do it jointly with your spouse. Or your trust. But get your own account where you deposit your assets and no one else does—no commingling with the decision maker. No one but you (and/or your spouse) has access to these funds. When you call the custodian, you actually *want* them to put you through a little bit of a wringer, asking for key information so they know you really are "you"—Mr. or Ms. Client—who you say you are, not an impostor. This means you don't just get statements from the money manager's firm in your name—that's fine—but actual, monthly statements from the custodian too, showing assets *held in your name*.

You want an account in your name at a big-name, third-party, non-connected custodian who makes you jump through hoops a little bit to confirm you are who you say you are. That shouldn't annoy you—that should give you confidence others won't be able to get at your money.

Your decision maker can have a limited power of attorney to direct investments. This is normal. But what they absolutely cannot ever do, and what you must never let them do, is request or make distributions or shift assets in or out of the custodian. Not ever. And by setting up your own account in your name at a third-party custodian, that can't happen if you don't let it. You put the money at the custodian.

Your separate money manager or financial adviser gets the right to buy and sell stocks at that custodian for your account but has no authority to take money outside and away from the custodian (unless authorized by you). Your custodian safe keeps you from your decision maker.

Maybe this precaution sounds silly. Of course you'd only open an account in your name, right? Let's hope so. Remember Mr. Wright— he bilked $185 million. This is what Joe Forte, Nicholas Cosmo, and Martin Frankel all did. They used commingled assets in plain vanilla accounts to steal hundreds of millions.

## Always a Red Flag?

Separating decision maker and custody and not commingling assets is rock-solid protection against most would-be scamsters. Unfortunately, it precludes investing in many hedge funds, venture capital, private equity investments, and other alternate investments that typically commingle assets. That might mean giving up some potential upside. Bear in mind, hedge funds, private equity, etc., aren't all upside and no downside—these vehicles can also be very risky. Just so happens they often have the additional risk inherent in commingled assets.

This doesn't mean all hedge fund managers are bad or intend to steal. Not at all. I know they don't. But if they really care about clients, they should protect them. Note: Many hedge funds could park assets in a non-connected custodian and not commingle. And some do—this is almost always safer for clients. There are reasons some don't. The entities they invest in will find the accounting costs of tracking all those separate accounts costly and annoying. But, if you're getting paid 2 percent a year and 20 percent of the profits as most hedge funds are, there is plenty of profit to cover these accounting costs.

In some cases, hedge fund managers want to buy securities that are tough to buy with smaller pools of assets or aren't easily accessible to individual investors through a plain-vanilla brokerage fund—like commodities, futures, or some derivatives. Fair enough. As long as you undertake rigorous due diligence this may be an appropriate risk worth taking. Up to you. But you need to know you still have a risk.

What about mutual funds? Say you have an account at Nationally Known Broker-Dealer, and the salesperson pitches Nationally Known brand mutual fund. Isn't that a decision-maker in direct contact with the assets? Maybe, but usually not—but always, *always* check. Most, if not all, of the larger mutual funds deposit client assets in a completely separate bank or trust company. Why? They wisely want to mitigate any potential conflicts of interest. You can see that clearly delineated in the mutual fund's prospectus. (A separate question is whether that salesperson receives a larger fee for selling the "house" mutual fund, and if that's a conflict of interest—but that's a topic for another book and isn't an embezzlement issue.)

# Further Reading

There aren't books on all the rats (and alleged ones) we've mentioned, but for further reading on some of history's most notorious, try these.

## MEET THE EMBEZZLERS

- *Ponzi's Scheme: The True Story of a Financial Legend* by Mitchell Zuckoff (Random House 2006).
- *Ponzi: The Incredible True Story of the King of Financial Cons* by Donald Dunn (Broadway 2004).
- *Vesco: From Wall Street to Castro's Cuba The Rise, Fall, and Exile of the King of White Collar Crime* by Arthur Herzog (IUniverse 2003).
- *The Match King: Ivar Kreuger, The Financial Genius Behind a Century of Wall Street Scandals* by Frank Partnoy (Public Affairs 2009).
- *Kreuger's Billion Dollar Bubble* by Earl Sparling (1932).
- *The Pretender: How Martin Frankel Fooled the Financial World and Led the Feds on One of the Most Publicized Manhunts in History* by Ellen Pollock (Free Press 2002).

And if you'd like more general reading on financial fraudsters through history, these are a good start.

## FRAUDSTERS THROUGH HISTORY

- *The Founding Finaglers* by Nathan Miller. This excellent 1976 book, not currently in print, can be found easily on eBay, Amazon.com, or in your favorite used bookstore.
- *Once in Golconda: A True Drama of Wall Street 1920–1938* by John Brooks (Wiley 1999).
- *The Big Con: The Story of the Confidence Man*, David Maurer (Anchor 1999).
- *The Embezzler*, Louis Auchincloss (1966). A spot-on work of fiction that's worth buying used.
- *100 Minds That Made the Market* by yours truly. That book isn't just about embezzlers, though I have a hefty section on some of history's biggest financial con artists (part of which is excerpted at the back of this book). This book walks you through 100 cameo biographies of folks who contributed hugely to America's capital markets, some for good and, like the rats, some for bad.

CHAPTER RECAP

# How Not to Be a Fraud Victim

In almost all situations, and in almost 100 percent of future scams, you can avoid having your funds "Madoff" with by *separating, entirely, your decision maker and the custody/safekeeping of your assets.*

This means you should:

- Insist your assets be deposited in a third-party, credible, large custodial institution with 24/7 Internet access.
- Insist your assets be held in a separate account in your name alone (or jointly with your spouse, or your trust).
- Never hire a discretionary money manager who holds assets at a broker-dealer he/she/it owns or controls.
- Never allow your assets to be commingled.

How can you make sure your decision maker doesn't have access? Easy. If the firm is registered, they must state whether they have custody on their Form ADV (a standard form all Registered Investment Advisors [RIAs]—which includes almost all forms of money managers and financial advisers—must file and update regularly). You can search for the ADV at www.adviserinfo.sec.gov. (More in Chapter 5.) Look for "Item 9"—you want your adviser to answer "No" to the questions relating to custody.

But if you aren't in front of a computer, here are a few key questions.

**Table 1.1**   Questions to Ask Your Adviser About Custody

| Question | Right Answer | Red Flag Answer |
|---|---|---|
| Where do I deposit funds? | With your third-party, big-name, nationally known, big-pocketed custodian. | With us! With my firm's affiliate In my firm's brokerage account. |
| Can I give my check to you? | No. We never take custody of your assets. Please send it to your custodian. | Yes. |
| How are you related to this institution? | Other than depositing other client assets there, we're not associated or affiliated at all. | We *are* the broker-dealer. They are an affiliate. |

---

CHAPTER RECAP *(CONTINUED)*

| Do I have online account access? | Yes, you have 24/7 online access through your custodian. | No.<br>Yes, but only through my firm's website. |
| Can I contact the custodian myself? | Yes, anytime. | You can contact us. |
| Who sends me statements? | In addition to any account information we send you, you'll also receive normal brokerage statements, monthly, directly from your custodian. | We do. |

---

If you must hire a money manager in some way connected to a custodian (because nothing is absolute, there can be reasons to combine the functions), make sure it's a big-name, big-pocketed firm with online access. Should your money manager go rogue, the odds of recouping losses are better with a big-pocketed firm, particularly if it's SIPC-insured. (My recommendation to RIAs is to always avoid custody— keeps life simpler. Good fences make good neighbors on both sides of the fence.)

Keep in mind, if your adviser "inflates" account values, even at a big SIPC-insured broker, they aren't necessarily responsible for restitution on the faked up amount. You could always sue for that, of course, which is why you want a big-pocketed firm. But it's pretty tough to prove you're entitled to fake portfolio returns, no matter how black-hearted the evil-doer was. To be fair, in the age of 24/7 account access, inflating account values the way Frank Gruttadauria did would be pretty tough— particularly for vigilant clients. But someone may figure out how to do it again. To be safe, keep the decision maker and assets separate—always.

# Chapter 2

# Too Good to Be True Usually Is

Jim sits down with a Trusty Time sales rep. First things first: He wants to know their performance. The Trusty Time rep says they don't try to knock the ball out of the park. Instead, they're "conservative." They get steady, reliable returns every year. They'd rather have smaller positive returns every year than wow with huge but volatile returns. Jim doesn't want wow, he wants steady.

Jim looks at their 15-year history. Never less than 8 percent, never more than 12 percent—they average about 10 percent overall. Jim thinks that's pretty steady and reasonable. He'd like to get bigger, market-beating returns, but maybe it's time to be more conservative. Ten percent is about what stocks average long term, and he'd be fine with that. And it seems almost too good to be true he could reach his goals and not have to suffer down years. He'd like that.

Jim's missed financial fraud sign number two and an almost universal truth—in investing and otherwise: If it seems too good to be true, it probably is. Look for the bad years that demonstrate integrity—because they do.

## Sign #2    Returns Are Consistently Great! Almost Too Good to Be True.

Every great money manager has had bad years. Even Warren Buffett. It's seeing the bad years, out front and in the open in the history of their returns, that makes you know they're real. Honest money managers and decision makers aren't ashamed of admitting their bad years or admitting mistakes. In my 2006 book, *The Only Three Questions That Count*, I documented that the most legendary investors of all time have only been right about 70 percent of the time. That means they were wrong about 30 percent of the time. Unfortunately, that rightness and wrongness often tends to come in clumpy patches that, at the time, can feel like they go on forever. But investing is a probabilities activity not a certainties activity, and being wrong 30 percent of the time is a perfectly marvelous success rate.

Then, too, the extended clumpy patches where an adviser is right year after year or wrong for over a year show up in the history of their returns, but neither are individually predictive of the manager's long-term past or future ability to manage money and get above-average results. Said another way: Above-average returns in the long term come with individual years that stink. And you need to accept that because it is in seeing the stinking years that you know a manager is actually honest.

### Where Are the Whoppers?

Con artists never display bad years. They just don't. Their returns are too good to be true because, by definition, they aren't true. Bad years scare daunted investors away and give them a clear sense that lightning can strike. They hate lightning. Con artists know that and give them what they want—smooth, never scary return displays. Someday, a rat will figure out how to package a return display that includes bad years to fake integrity while somehow packaging it so it doesn't scare fearful investors away; but it hasn't come out of the woodwork yet.

An amazing feature about the more egregious recent frauds is how long they lasted. Madoff operated for 20 years—possibly record-breaking for a "successful" Ponzi. "Sir" Stanford's long (alleged) con rivaled that. Joseph Forte bilked victims for $50 million since at least 1995.[1] Nicholas Cosmo managed to operate long enough to allegedly steal approximately $370 million.[2] Kirk Wright lasted 10 years and took maybe $185 million.[3]

How can a con last that long, putting aside regulatory concerns? They don't do it by reporting believable returns with a number of scary down years among their history. The down years would make people know they have to be careful about when to get out. Con artists don't want them to ever think about getting out because they don't want to have to come up with new money from other investors to pay them off. That new money is extra work, and when they can't find it to pay off the departing investor, they know they'll be caught.

Fraudsters claim not just fake returns, but fake returns that are consistently high, positive, and better than what you could get normally from markets—no matter what stocks, bonds, or other principle securities do.

Doesn't matter how they claim to do it. Some claim flashy tactics (more in Chapter 3), proprietary trading techniques, options, commodities, futures, real estate, loans—whatever. There is nothing wrong with any of those things. But whatever an investor may use to invest, make no mistake, fraudsters will claim a high annualized return from it, higher than long-term equity averages, higher than commodity or real estate returns, and varying little year to year. Their stated return history tends to be very non-volatile, smooth, soft, and dream-like—the very image of return without risk, which is what everyone wants, deep down.

People don't like volatility. You don't like volatility. I think Warren Buffett is about the only guy I've ever seen to openly claim he likes volatility.

Those with the optimal mentality to be conned (see Chapter 1) particularly don't like volatility, which is why the swindler claims non-volatile returns. As much as consistently market-beating positive returns each and every year sound nice, that's almost as big a red flag as an adviser with full access to your money.

I can't say this enough: Look for the bad years. If there aren't some doozies, go elsewhere. Those bad years could be in terms of absolute returns or relative returns, but there need to be some whoppers because everyone who is honest has whoppers. A year like 2008, when markets freefell, is a perfectly logical year to see an honest manager have dismal numbers. The world stock market was down 41 percent,[4] so anyone that didn't get out of the market is very likely to have had big absolute losses of a scary size.

But the whopper could happen in any other year. Maybe the manager makes a couple of big bets that were exactly backwards and wrong. So in a year like 2007, when the global stock market was up 9 percent,[5] maybe his returns are down 15 percent because he made huge bets on banks and consumer discretionary stocks that did badly then. That 15 percent bad year, lagging the market terribly, is a sign of integrity. Real con artist rats will never show that. Their numbers are lulling, smooth, perfect. You don't want to see a lot of years when the manager did terribly, but everyone that's been around a long time has at least one. Look for it.

## The High Return Opiate

While depositing money in an account linked to the decision maker is the con's basic structure, stunning phony performance numbers are the honey used to ensnare and lull victims. Some cons can lull you for years!

When the Madoff news hit, folks asked, "Why didn't the SEC stop him?" One reason— he wasn't registered until 2006. Another: Clients don't complain about huge returns and particularly not about a manager who generates great returns even in bad times. Madoff's clients believed they were getting the returns he was claiming. They never had a clue it was all phony baloney.

And on the SEC: Fact is they're overworked, understaffed, and no matter what, in any given year, they can only inspect a small percentage of the many money managers that exist. They couldn't get around to all of them in a five-year period if they had to—impossible. All else being equal, it would make sense the SEC is more likely to inspect managers with a lot of complaints filed by customers. But those, ironically, are mostly on the honest managers who happened to have a bad year that clients saw and complained about. And when the SEC inspects an honest manager who had a bad year and lots of complaints, it won't find anything very terrible except a straight-up manager who didn't see the markets right. That's no crime and that's something the client can bounce back from in future years.

The SEC doesn't get a lot of complaints from the rats' clients because the rats keep fooling the clients into thinking they've got nothing to complain about. The clients just don't complain and the firm isn't number one on the SEC's radar. In fact, Madoff's clients adored him and considered themselves super lucky to be in his "club." Why would they complain?

Con artists use claims of great, non-volatile, consistently positive returns to ensnare victims and keep them docile. And fake returns help stall detection. Who complains about returns that are up big, no matter what the market does?

### Don't Complain; Won't Redeem

Scamsters know investors who think they're getting great results won't complain. More important, enough won't redeem—letting assets ride—compounding the great (fake) return rate. If investors in-and-out fast, a pyramid scheme collapses faster. But if you think you're getting 15 percent *each and every year*—little volatility—you're likely to let it ride and not withdraw assets—as many Madoff investors did.

If a few investors redeem or take periodic distributions, these can be supported in normal Ponzi fashion—new money pays off older investors as they redeem. The fake high return keeps attracting new money, new victims, new suckers—all sizes. A fraudster skilled and charismatic enough can avoid detection for years, compounding losses, creating a wider victim web. And the longer the pyramid runs, the more desperate the con gets for new money. And remember, a con artist doesn't only want big-monied victims—a dollar's a dollar, and any amount helps support the con.

## Claw-Back Crisis

When the pyramid collapses, inflated values hurt investors two ways. First—most obviously—they've lost money. Second, they believe their losses to be much more than they would be in a legit vehicle. Say over the scam's 10 years you believe your money's increased 10-fold—you think your $100,000 has become $1 million! You feel like the thief stole $1 million. Doesn't matter if that amount, invested normally, would have grown much less—or maybe sustained a loss. You *thought* you had $1 million, so it *feels* like a $1 million loss. You based the rest of your life on the supposition of having that $1 million—doesn't matter if it was fake the whole time. This is why it took courts so long to figure how much Chapter 1's Frank Gruttadauria stole, and why it's taken a while for the custodians to pay restitution. How can you know just what to pay when accounts had been fiction for 15 years?

An additional wrinkle? Many of Madoff's victims—including charities—took distributions, sometimes worth many times what they initially invested, believing they were rightful profits. These victims—insult to injury—may face "claw backs" as authorities try retrieving falsely gotten gains to help restore other victims.[6]

This is a concept known in the law with the misleading title of "fraudulent conveyance." It makes it sound as if the person or entity that got the distribution based on phony baloney had committed some form of fraud, which isn't true. Still, it is true that the supposed paid-out profits weren't really profits at all and were central to the fraud. It is common in the legal process for the most recent victims to have some success in clawing back some of those payouts from earlier investors. But those profits were, in many cases, long spent to cover operating costs, living expenses, etc.

Imagine how you would feel if you had put in a million dollars (or $10,000 or $10 million) and gotten 5 percent back in distributions each year. And the account supposedly grew even more than that as the scamster claimed high returns. So you collected while the account (in your mind) grew and grew—for years. And then you find out you have nothing in your account. Then you're told by some court on the other side of the country to pay back all the 5 percent dividends you got, which you spent, long ago, with good intent. Simply: It's a terrible mess. Where are you going to get that money to pay back to the court?

That's why you want to make sure this never happens to you.

## How High Is Too High?

Since many money managers have a stated goal of aiming to "beat the market," how do you tell a good manager achieving good long-term goals from a potential fraud at work? Can't good returns just mean good management? Sure! To separate an honest operator from a con, look for one of two things:

1. Eerie consistency year to year, or
2. Average returns *hugely* beating long-term stock averages.

Some fraudsters claim eerie consistency—little variance. They won't wow with super-outsized returns. Rather, they say they're *conservative*— don't try to beat the market by much. They're consistent. Markets up 35 percent? They're up 10 to 12 percent. But when markets drop 35 percent, they'll still be up 10 to 12 percent. I've got nothing against someone who legitimately manages money with a style that generates those returns, but it is a red flag. If they claim these kinds of returns, you want to be extra special sure they don't have custody of your money as per Chapter 1.

This was Madoff's game—he claimed 10 to 12 percent every year. Stanford was the same—he reported 15.71 percent returns for 1995 and 1996—*identical to a hundredth of a basis point*! He reported positive returns throughout the 2000 to 2003 big bear market, and claimed to only be down 1.3 percent in 2008—a year global stocks were down 41 percent.[7] Many Madoff and Stanford investors reported they thought they were being conservative by not demanding hugely market-beating returns!

Such consistency is a super red flag. Investing with high returns is not a consistent process. It just isn't. A money market fund probably consistently returns a few percent each year—that's perfectly normal and fine. It invests in fairly non-volatile assets. But consistent 10 percent annual returns, regardless of what the market does, are usually a fairy tale. That's not how markets behave. Long term, stocks have averaged about 10 percent annually, depending on when you measure. But that *average* includes wildly varying annual returns.

The best in the business, who *do* have actual long-term records beating the market, don't have consistent returns. Bill Miller is a long-time, super-successful mutual fund manager. He had, until a few years ago, a long run of consistently beating his benchmark each year—the S&P 500. But he didn't have consistently positive returns. Sometimes he beat only marginally, others he beat by a wide margin. Lots of variability. He had years he was up 20 percent, 30 percent, and more. And he had big down years, too—like the market. *Beating the market doesn't mean always positive*. Beating the market means beating the market—if

---

## A Gentleman's Game

It appears Madoff didn't just have suspiciously steady investing returns. He applied the same strategy to reporting golf scores—always between 80 and 89. What does this tell you? Well, a basic rule is that cheats and liars tend to cheat and lie in multiple arenas, not just one.

Source: Mark Seal, "Madoff's World," *Vanity Fair* (April 2009).

the market's down 35 percent, being down 25 percent is still beating the market by a whole lot.

And though Bill Miller had a great run, he's run into a patch of seriously bad years—down and lagging the S&P 500 badly. That doesn't mean now he's a bad manager. It means he had a long spate of great years and was due for some bad ones. Happens to the best of them. My firm has a long-term history beating both the S&P 500 and the MSCI World Indexes in all-equity portfolios,* but we've had years we're down big, similar to the market in 2008. And we've had years we've lagged our benchmark. That's the truth, we don't hide it, but it doesn't mean we won't or can't still beat the market over time. And we're certainly not positive every year! You can't realistically aim to beat an equity benchmark and be positive every year. Simply can't happen.

But note, Bill Miller is pretty much the only guy who had consistent back-to-back-to-back market-beating individual years. And his returns weren't similar year to year—and he had big down years! Consistent, year-in-year-out, positive returns close to or beating long-term stock averages are simply too good to be true—and usually aren't. Period. Don't believe anyone telling you otherwise. A fraudster relies on victims who either don't know or suspend their disbelief. Arming yourself with market history can help combat fraudsters. Know what the S&P 500 and world stocks did historically. Find it on any finance web site. If a manager shows annual performance of 10 percent, 12 percent, 11 percent, and 12 percent when you know stocks did 40 percent, 24 percent, –28 percent, and 7 percent, tell him, "Sorry Charlie! Makes no sense," and take your money elsewhere.

---

*The Fisher Investments Private Client Group (FI PCG) Global Total Return (GTR) strategy was incepted on January 1, 1995 and is managed against the Morgan Stanley Capital International (MSCI) World Index. For the period from inception through December 31, 2008, performance returns (net of advisory fees, commissions and other expenses, and reflecting the reinvestment of dividends and other earnings) of the FI PCG GTR composite have exceeded total returns of the MSCI World Index as well as the S&P 500 Index. Past performance is no guarantee of future returns. Investing in stock markets involves the risk of loss.

Consistent returns year to year are suspicious, as are wildly above-average returns. Much as everyone would like an account that's up big every year, regardless of the market, this is a bad sign.

## Big Returns, Bold Con Artists

At least a 10 percent average return is reasonable to believe. (Remember —*average* return, over long periods. Not 10 percent each and every year.) Some scammers make detection easier—theoretically—by claiming preposterously high returns. Nicholas Cosmo claimed 48 percent *annual* returns![8] Arthur Nadel claimed 11 to 12 percent returns *per month* throughout 2008.[9] Daren Palmer claimed 40 percent annual returns. Charles Ponzi himself promised returns as high as 50 percent over 90 days.[10] Sounds ridiculous—but clearly enough folks were convinced and bamboozled. These cons collected *millions* from investors. Of course, Ponzi didn't last as long as Madoff just because his very high and unbelievable return claims attracted the attention of the *Boston Post*, who outed him. The *Boston Post* figured out he had to be phony—they knew his returns were too good to be true so they told the whole world.

Can an adviser do 50 percent in one year? Sure! Happens all the time! Two years in a row? Sure! But returns consistently beating the market by so wide a margin? Suspicious and almost certainly impossible. And an adviser can never promise future returns. Past performance is no guarantee of future returns—ever. Even if an adviser's had stellar past returns, he, she, or it can't promise they'll repeat. All they can say is they'll stick to a strategy they believe is superior. How that impacts future performance is up to the fickle market and their skill. Any return guarantee is an additional huge red flag—by law, advisers can't promise future returns. But con artists tend not to be fastidious about securities laws.

Again, know your market history. If stocks are up 40 percent, and your adviser was up 80 percent, maybe that's legit. Maybe a huge bet paid off. Happens all the time! But if your adviser claims to consistently beat by so much, know your adviser is either taking massive risk that can definitely go the other way, or they could be fabricating returns. If the former, consider if that much risk is appropriate for you. If the latter, take your money—if there's any left—and run.

# How to Tell a Pro From a Con

Everyone puts their best foot forward when selling anything, right? Including money management services. How can you tell a fraud from an honest adviser who wants your business? Easy, the honest adviser can't hide past bad performance and won't try to. Pretty much every adviser who's been in the business long enough will have sour years— one (or two or more!) when the market was down big and they were too, or years they lagged by a little or a lot because market bets didn't work. That's ok! That's better. A con artist will sell all sunshine. You don't want sunshine only—you want reality. Let a little rain drizzle into your life.

The difference between a legit adviser and a scamster is that a legitimate pro will:

- Manage to some stated benchmark of some form you can understand.
- Have a reasonable record of past performance.
- Explain deviations from the benchmark that link to overall strategy.

## State Your Benchmark

First, your manager should have a stated benchmark. If your adviser (or potential adviser) makes loose claims about "beating the market," ask "Which market is that?"

Professional equity managers typically pick an index—the "market" —as their benchmark. The index is usually easy to follow in financial papers or online—the S&P 500, the MSCI World Index, the Russell 2000, the EAFE, NASDAQ, etc. Whether the benchmark is all equity, all fixed income, a blend, or some other market index, this is the bar they set in measuring performance.

If a manager doesn't have a stated benchmark, or it shifts around, do additional digging—that could be a bad sign. Or it could be a sign they don't manage to a benchmark and instead try to maximize absolute return every year—hit it out of the park. Maximizing absolute return can lead to maximizing risk—which can lead to outsized losses. That may not be appropriate for many investors and may or may not be appropriate for you. (For more on why a benchmark is a useful tool in managing portfolio risk, see my 2006 book *The Only Three Questions That Count.*)

See it this way: Madoff didn't have a benchmark. Neither did Stanford. How could they? No index returns 10 to 12 percent each and every year. If one existed, every adviser would invest using it. Cosmo and Forte didn't have benchmarks—they picked wild numbers and hoped enough victims bought it. A benchmark gives you a reasonable basis to judge advisers against and clues you in to wild—possibly suspicious—performance variations.

## A Reasonable Record

Not only should the manager disclose a benchmark up front, they should provide performance history (i.e., not word of mouth from other investors). Performance history from a legit manager generally comes with a slew of legalese and disclosures. If you see performance claims not followed by sufficient disclosures, something is likely afoot. The disclosures are there to detail how the returns were measured and calculated (i.e., how composites were constructed consistent with the rules for so doing).

Many larger RIAs now use Global Investment Performance Standards (GIPS®) when reporting performance—simply because many larger, institutional investors started demanding it in recent years. Created by the CFA Institute, GIPS give standardized, industry-wide guidance on performance calculation and reporting. If firms report using GIPS, you can compare apples to apples and know exactly how and why the firm reports historic performance and exactly why it does it that way. Using GIPS isn't mandatory for money managers, so if a

## Double Your Money Guaranteed!

You've likely received emails with jaw-dropping claims: "Double your money buying these stocks!" "If you bought the stocks I recommended, you'd be up 400 percent!" And so on. Can you believe them?

Categorically, no. It may be true that one stock a newsletter writer touted ran up 400 percent, but they usually tout many stocks—no doubt a few are big winners. They almost never advertise upfront how their big losers did or how their stock picks did overall. This is radically different from how advisers advertise. They just can't say "If you'd hired me, you would have held stock ABC that is up 600 percent!" That's not the full picture.

Note, most newsletter writers' core business is selling newsletter subscriptions. Touting their big winners helps sell newsletters. But that's likely not remotely close to a good representation of how you would have done had you followed their prescribed strategy.

There is nothing wrong with the notion of newsletters. The point: Wild, sensational claims from someone who is going to take your money is a huge red flag. Simply said, advertising outsized performance is exactly how Charles Ponzi started his Ponzi scheme. Don't fall for it.

money manager doesn't use them, it's not a negating factor. But GIPS can be another useful due diligence tool. (For more on GIPS, go to www.gipsstandards.org.)

### Performance Irregularities

With the benchmark and the performance history, you can measure whether an adviser does a consistently good job or not. You want them to perform close to the benchmark, most of the time—that's a sign of an adviser doing a good job. This may sound strange, but if your manager's benchmark is down 25 percent and they aren't, they have some serious explaining to do. There may well be a good, simple explanation, but you want to know what it is. And it needs to make sense.

This again requires you to know your history. If your manager has a benchmark, check what it did historically (on any finance web site) and compare. In most years, your manager should perform pretty close to their benchmark—maybe a relative few percent over or under. If their benchmark is down a lot and they aren't—could be perfectly legitimate! But have them explain how. What did they know? How did they forecast it? What did they see others didn't? If the explanation links to their overall portfolio strategy and the way they've managed money in the past, that's good! If it was a wild guess gone right, that's less good, but not criminal. Lucky is ok, but the next wild guess might not be as lucky. If they have no explanation or a murky one—or one you can't understand—that's a bad sign.

You want an adviser to perform relatively similar to their benchmark. Wild deviations could signal excess risk-taking, or something far worse.

Wild performance irregularity may not signal fraud—not at all! In fact, if the returns are wildly volatile it almost certainly indicates the lack of an embezzler. Remember: Big, consistently positive returns with no downside sound great. Unfortunately, such performance isn't sustainable long term. If you want market-like returns, you must accept market-like volatility, most of the time. If you want more consistent returns, you must accept lower annualized averages. No other way to say that.

## The Plain Truth

It's just a fact: Most pros fail to beat their benchmarks over long periods. There are a few, very successful pros who have done it. And even they don't beat it each and every year. They have individual years that they lag—sometimes a few in a row. Does that mean the pros who can't beat the market are terrible? No—it just means it's very, very hard to do.

Most professionals lag markets over time. You know that. But most individual investors do even worse and actually by a lot. An excellent study by Dalbar Associates tracked individual investor behavior and performance. Over the 20 years ending December 31, 2007, the S&P 500 index returned an annualized average 11.8 percent. But equity mutual fund investors on average got only an annualized 4.5 percent.[11]

Why did they do so badly when it's easy to buy the S&P 500 as a passive index and let it ride? Because it *isn't* easy to buy the S&P 500 and let it ride! Investors can't take their hands off the steering wheels of their bumper cars and let their feet off the gas and the brake, so they swerve in and out of the market at the wrong times, and get a much lower return than the market itself generates.

Many investors rationally know they should turn a hard shoulder to near-term volatility and be tough—but emotions take over. They make active decisions to avoid near-term pain at the expense of longer-term returns. In behavioral finance, this is called *myopic loss aversion*—and it can cause costly errors. Passive isn't easy—it's hard. Few can stomach it.

During periods of increased volatility—even during normal bull market corrections—it's typical to see investors become fearful. They fear equities will no longer get the long-term averages they once did. This is where the saying "bull markets climb a wall of worry" comes from. Investors want less volatility—more stability. Once spooked out of equities, many investors don't return—not for years and maybe not ever. They wait for a world that's more clear. Clarity in markets, of course, always comes at a high price, so they hop out of stocks and don't return until they're sure the market is rebounding—missing big early returns and materially impacting long-term averages—as the Dalbar study showed! This happens regularly in every market downturn and is the main reason investors on average lag the market so badly.

Most long-term investors agree staying long-term focused and not fretting short-term volatility is best. But empirically, many can't do it—not on their own. It's hard! Which is why advisers—even those who don't have market-beating averages—can help by keeping investors long-term focused instead of caving to myopic loss aversion and hurting themselves worse.

### Beware the Midas Touch

Maybe fraudsters will wise up in the future and start reporting normal-sounding, volatile, and realistic performance—though it's hard to imagine them doing that. They need huge and steady "returns" to attract big sums and keep clients docile so none upset the scam too early. Regardless of performance, always do thorough due diligence. But dig deeper if your adviser seemingly has a magic touch.

Ask your adviser (or the one you're considering hiring) to show you a bad year—one they were down big, either because the market was too or perhaps because they lagged their benchmark by a lot. Ask what went wrong and what they learned from it. Learning from past mistakes is ok. My father used to love quoting Herbert H. Dow, founder of Dow Chemical, who said, "Never promote a man who hasn't made some bad mistakes. You would be promoting someone who hasn't done much." Maybe your manager never had a bad or down year, but I'd argue someone who hasn't been through a bad patch or two hasn't been managing money long enough to be very skilled—and doesn't know emotionally how to react when it does eventually happen.

## Average Returns Aren't Normal; Normal Returns Are Extreme

Some folks have a hard time differentiating between a thief and a portfolio that's down a lot. You used to have a million, now you have half a million. What's the difference between that and a thief stealing half your money?

An entire universe. Market volatility is normal—even big volatility like in 2008 into 2009. Investing in securities involves the risk of loss—period. Single stocks can and do get halved overnight—or go to zero! That's not a sign of illegality—it's just a sign of normal risk in an asset class that's historically delivered superior long-term returns.

Don't mistake normal market volatility for financial fraud. Volatility is normal—if you want market-like returns, you want market-like volatility, most of the time. Without volatility, you likely get lower returns over time.

Can a stock dropping big be a sign of illegality? Sure—think Enron or WorldCom. In those cases, upper management engaged in illegal accounting practices to fool shareholders, regulators, and the public. But those cases are fortunately rare and involve single stocks, not managed money of any form. Market volatility, however, isn't rare. Perfectly healthy single stocks can experience wild price swings—in good economic times and bad. And markets correct hugely—in both bull and bear markets.

Folks have a hard time getting in their bones that stocks don't remotely return 10 percent each year. They go down big and up bigger. Simply: Average returns aren't normal—normal returns are extreme. Table 2.1 shows annual returns for the S&P 500 (because US stocks have the most historic data) broken into return ranges and occurrences. A surprising feature—if you take big returns and negative returns together they happen a lot more often than "average" returns. Average returns just aren't normal. In fact, stocks are up big—meaning in excess of 20 percent—37 percent of the time. They've been negative 29 percent of the time. But they've only been in the 0 to 20 percent range a third of all years. Two-thirds of all years they're up big or negative. Normal returns are extreme.

Interestingly, since 1926, stocks have had an annual return that was very close to its long-term average (between 9 and 11 percent) merely three times: 1968, 1993, and 2004. It's just not normal for stocks to have an *average* year—but that's what many scamsters want you to believe because it would feel good! If you looked at Madoff and knew it was bizarre for stocks to return around 10 percent every year, you would know his claimed return history was bizarre and you more likely wouldn't have hired him. Those who hired him didn't figure this out and suffered for it.

Table 2.1    Average Returns Aren't Normal; Normal Returns Are Extreme

| S&P 500 Annual Return Range | | | Occurrences Since 1926 | Frequency | |
|---|---|---|---|---|---|
| | > | 40% | 5 | 6.0% | ⎫ |
| 30% | to | 40% | 13 | 15.7% | ⎬ Big Returns 37.3% |
| 20% | to | 30% | 13 | 15.7% | ⎭ |
| 10% | to | 20% | 16 | 19.3% | ⎫ |
| 0% | to | 10% | 12 | 14.5% | ⎬ Average Returns 33.7% |
| –10% | to | 0% | 12 | 14.5% | ⎫ |
| –20% | to | –10% | 6 | 7.2% | |
| –30% | to | –20% | 3 | 3.6% | ⎬ Negative Returns 28.9% |
| –40% | to | –30% | 2 | 2.4% | |
| | < | –40% | 1 | 1.2% | ⎭ |
| **Total Occurrences** | | | 83 | | |
| **Simple Average** | | | 11.6% | | |
| **Annualized Average** | | | 9.5% | | |

Global Financial Data as of 12/31/08

Remember, stocks' long-term averages *include* big down years. During periods of big downside volatility, I've heard folks say, "I'm down huge! I'll never make it back!" They make a common cognitive error—expecting markets to deliver measured returns each year. If markets returned about 10 percent each year, and you're down 40 percent or 50 percent or more, it would indeed take years to regain past highs. But that's not how markets typically behave—look at Table 2.1 again. There's no way to predict how long it takes for markets to recoup steep losses, but it's likely far faster than most presume, and then stocks typically climb to fresh highs. Always been that way.

Some bearish folks like to say stocks are perpetually in a "secular bear market"—meaning stocks' long-term trend is negative. That may sell newsletter subscriptions or get you on CNBC, but think about it. Logically, it doesn't make sense! Look at a chart of the long-term history of the stock market and immediately it's clear that doesn't make sense. Stocks tend to rise more than fall over time.

Equities are likeliest to give superior returns long term—but it's never been a smooth ride. This is the exact opposite of what Madoff, Stanford, and hundreds of con artists claim. Scamsters want victims to believe big positive returns are possible with no down years. They're not.

Someone selling you market-like or better returns with no downside is almost certainly a con artist.

Fact is: Folks who suffer the slings and arrows of big market volatility and see their portfolios hammered by a bear market *still have capital* to enjoy the next bull market. Even those who panic and sell at relative market lows—buy high and sell low—still have something to invest again, however wisely or foolishly they choose. But, sadly, folks who are cheated by con artists end up with nothing at all.

Unfortunately, perfectly normal market volatility can make people seek perceived "safer" returns—sometimes getting them into trouble. Just remember: ***If someone sells you on getting market-like or better returns and never experiencing a negative year—run away! This almost certainly is a scam.***

## Bear Punishment

Bear markets punish investors in myriad ways—most obviously by sending portfolio values down, near term. But what markets taketh away, they generally giveth back and then some with reasonable time. The tragedy of bear markets—or any period of steep volatility—is they cause otherwise rational people to do themselves harm.

Harm comes in many stripes. Folks may abandon a sound long-term strategy in favor of perceived near-term security. Many sell stocks at precisely the worst time—in effect buying high and selling low. Adding insult to injury, they then miss out on what's usually a fast, steep initial upswing of a new bull market. Miss that, and you can seriously impact your long-term return average.

But, ironically, it's this same tendency to want to get out and flee the market at and around its lows that uncovers most Ponzi schemes. When investors get most afraid and want to go to cash, they liquidate their investments in Ponzi schemes to get cash. When they do that, the Ponzi scheme can't cover the redemptions with new money because new investors are too afraid to put money into the market. No (or few) new investors and a flood of redemptions and the Ponzi operator can't pay off those departing and gets discovered for what he is. This is why most major Ponzi schemes get discovered late in a bear market or early in a new bull market. Pessimism is high and the scamster can't find new suckers to pay off the old suckers.

This is why there were so many swindlers uncovered in the back half of 2008 and early in 2009. The market decline created the pessimism that made their games unsustainable. You know that the 2008 to 2009 bear market was huge. But there's another way to see how huge it was: It was huge enough to finally stop Bernard Madoff after 20 years of Ponzi ratting. The 1990 bear market wasn't big enough to do it. The 1998 near-bear market wasn't big enough. And 2000 to 2002 wasn't big enough. But 2008 was. It was just that big.

And, just as ironically, the discovery of these Ponzi schemes then makes normal investors more pessimistic and more suspicious because they see all the ratty evil that is within and around us. Suddenly, they realize a different side of life than they had been thinking about recently and wonder if the guy next to them on the train in a suit with a briefcase is a swindler, if their brother-in-law is, or if their money manager is—and maybe they should sell and get their cash into a safe bank. The bear market uncovers the schemes, and the uncovering of the schemes makes investors more bearish.

Ultimately, this is all part of the process that makes a bear market culminate in pessimism that is oversold and rolls over into the beginning of the next bull market. That won't change. By the time we've ended the next bull market, we will have a new crop of swindlers to uncover. Always have been, always are, and always will be.

# Further Reading

Fraudsters love bamboozling with fake returns. Knowing how to correctly calculate investment returns can help you avoid a rat attack.

## Too Good to Be True No More

- *Investment Performance Measurement* by Bruce J. Feibel (Wiley 2003). This excellent textbook may be too technical for some, but it details the correct way to measure investment performance, as well as attribution, risk, etc.
- *How to Lie with Statistics* by Darrell Huff (W.W. Norton & Company 1954). This must-have classic helps you understand when someone's lying simply with straightforward statistics.

Knowing market performance history keeps you from being fooled. But knowing broader market history helps you frame realistic expectations.

## History Lessons

- *100 Years of Wall Street* by Charles R. Geisst (McGraw-Hill 2000).
- *The Wall Street Waltz: 90 Visual Perspectives, Illustrated Lessons from Financial Cycles and Trends* by Ken Fisher (Wiley 2007).
- *The Big Board: A History of the New York Stock Market* by Robert Sobel (Beard Books 2000). A reprint of the excellent, 1965 classic.
- *The Global Securities Market: A History* by Ranald Michie (Oxford University Press 2008). Rather pricey, but this text is global in view, and there are few good market history books that are.
- *A History of the Global Stock Market: From Ancient Rome to Silicon Valley* by B. Mark Smith (University of Chicago Press 2004). Another good global look at stock market history.

## CHAPTER RECAP

### Performance Prattle

Everyone wants great returns with no downside. But the truth is, big returns with no down years aren't possible. So how can you find a legit pro with a good long-term history as opposed to an embezzler with a good-looking fake history? First and foremost, hire someone non-connected to the custodian. Then ask:

- Do you manage to a benchmark? What is it?
- May I see past performance?
- Have you had a bad year? What went wrong?
- Have you had a great year when you far outperformed your benchmark? Why?

Your homework isn't done. Make sure you:

- Know your market history. Check what the adviser's benchmark has done historically and compare.
- Look for eerie consistency. A money market fund can get similar, relatively low returns year to year. But an adviser managing any amount of stocks should have greater year-to-year variability.
- Look for huge, consistently too-good-to-be-true returns, much better than what the benchmark did. This is a bad sign of either excess risk or something worse.

# Chapter 3

# Don't Be Blinded by Flashy Tactics

Next, Jim wants to know what Trusty Time will buy for him. He considers himself a dabbler and pretty darn smart, even though he doesn't have time to do this himself. The Trusty Time rep winks, "It's proprietary and pretty complicated."

Jim puffs up, "Try me! I took two semesters of Econ in college and have been managing my own portfolio for years." The Trusty rep nods solemnly and explains, "It's actually quite simple. We arbitrage away currency spreads in foreign options, focusing on lean metrics with reasonable valuations, embodied in high volumes by trading in foreign ordinaries while shorting stocks with low correlation to core portfolio holdings to reduce volatility and produce more reliable returns."

Jim gulps and nods, "Oh sure. I can see how that would work."

Jim's falling prey to financial fraud sign number three: Being blinded by flashy tactics and murky strategies.

## Sign #3 The Investing Strategy Isn't Understandable—Is Murky, Flashy, or "Too Complicated" for Him (Her, or It) to Describe So You Easily Understand

Con rats know precious few investors have spent much time deeply studying capital market intricacies. Most investors who hire professionals do so because living their lives—careers, families, hobbies—takes precedence. For many, advanced investing tactics can intimidate. Maybe to the point they won't ask questions—either because they assume the adviser is smarter, at least in investing, or because they don't want to seem like they aren't "in the know."

Not admitting you don't understand may save your ego, but it can eliminate all your money—110 percent of it. (The other 10 percent comes if you're silly enough to hire a lawyer to chase an embezzler as many are doing with Madoff and other embezzling rats, because at the end of that rainbow, there's simply no pot of gold. There's never anything to collect large enough relative to the costs of the litigation to make it worth doing. The money's long gone and, sadly, there's usually nothing to get back.)

Rats play on confusing strategies—intentionally aiming to confuse or intimidate—to keep clients from questioning them too closely. Don't fall for it—a non-rat adviser will never hesitate to simply and openly discuss strategy. Because a good strategy *should* be straightforward. If your adviser's strategy seems murky, and he can't or won't explain it more simply, or if they tout a string of flashy trading tactics, be suspicious—this is a common rat tactic.

For example, folks seemed endlessly shocked by Madoff. He seemed so avuncular—a pillar of society. But in most ways, he was a textbook rat. He took custody of assets. He reported "too good to be true" returns. And his investing strategy was completely inscrutable. There's no reason to not be as clear as possible—to actually aim to confuse—unless you're hiding a scam. A 2001 *Barron's* article (a full eight years before he was outed!) lifted this description of Madoff's strategy straight from his marketing materials:

> Typically, a position will consist of the ownership of 30 to 35 S&P 100 stocks, most correlated to that index, the sale of out-of-the-money calls on the index and the purchase of out-of-the-money puts on the index. The sale of the calls is designed to increase the rate of return, while allowing upward movement of the stock portfolio to the strike price of the calls. The puts, funded in large part by the sale of the calls, limit the portfolio's downside.[1]

Excuse me! But based on the performance he was claiming, finance theory says that is completely impossible, unless you have some underlying strategy for precisely timing put and call sales—in which case you don't even need the 30 to 35 S&P 100 stocks. (Which, by the way, constitute a third of the very biggest, most efficiently traded, and hardest to out-think-the-market US stocks. If there were ever a way to predict stock movements and that of their puts and calls relative to the market, it would least likely work on these stocks. But investors would probably be more comfortable thinking their investment is based on these stocks, which is why it worked for Madoff-the-Rat.) This is no "underlying" strategy; it's just a lying strategy. In the long term, put and call prices for the biggest, most liquid stocks by definition must offset each other. They're the flip sides of the same coin and therefore there's no way in hell the puts can be "funded in large part by the sale of the calls."

A strategy to time sales of puts and calls is, by definition, no different than timing trades of the underlying stocks. And if Madoff had such a strategy, why wasn't he talking about it and why weren't his clients and prospective clients asking him about it? If I had a strategy that could do that consistently, I'd own the world in no time at all. So would you, and you would never think about hiring Madoff or anyone else to handle your money because you would be the world's best at it yourself. This was nut-job, mumbo-jumbo talk from the get-go, aimed to appeal to folks who never took Stock Market 101 in high school.

But even if that weren't so, the strategy statement itself is enough to make most prospective investors a little cross-eyed—which in my view was exactly the intent. If a strategy or tactic confuses, don't assume the manager is smarter. Assume they either can't explain themselves well—a bad sign—or it's something more sinister—a quite terrible sign.

It is central to all con artists that you not understand, because if you did, you would never give them your money. Certain folks have a long history of waving their wands over your face to convince you that you can't and shouldn't try to understand. Some of those folks, usually perfectly honest and reputable men and women, are in every field from medicine to law to politics to education (ok, not politics, I was off base there)—but 100 percent of financial embezzlers do it. If you press them, they devolve to mumbo jumbo. If you get mumbo-jumbo answers, get leery. Look at Bernie's jive.

## Madoff's Big Con

Madoff, if pressed (because he reportedly demured from answering direct questions about his tactics), confessed to *split-strike conversions*.[2] Perhaps "split-strike conversion" sounded fancy, but there is no reason for the murky description—he could have just said "we buy collars" and then defined *collar* for investors newer to option investing.

### Split-Strike What?

For the mumbo-jumbo oriented reader: What exactly is a "split-strike conversion" (i.e., collar)? And how, if done correctly, does it work? Hypothetically, you buy ABC stock for $100. At the same time, you sell an ABC call option with a strike price of $110 and use the premium income to buy an ABC put option, strike price $90. (If you need a refresher on options, puts, calls, etc., try a website like Investopedia that gives basic descriptions for all things financial.)

Theoretically, downside is limited—if the stock falls below $90, the put option kicks in and the stock sells. Even if the stock falls to $1, you get to sell for $90 so you can't *lose* more than $10. Yippee! But you've also limited upside. If the stock rises above $110, the call option kicks in and you must also sell—you can't *make* more than $10. (Of course, there are transaction fees and taxes, but forget those for now. Bernie would!) If the stock wiggles and remains between $90 and $110 until the option expiration date, you just own a stock that hasn't done much.

The benefits? If you think markets will fall a lot, downside is limited. But, if you think markets will fall a lot, you could just hold cash and/or bonds or even sell short and not futz around with options and inherently higher transaction costs. The drawbacks? Many. In a rising market, upside is capped, and you still have all those increased transactions, fees, taxes, etc., that we forgot.

Using collars isn't necessarily a red flag. Some folks like them because you can't make or lose much. Personally, I think they're inefficient, costly, and there are a million better ways to skin that cat. And they're inherently a small-time, short-term timing game—or there is no game there at all. But to run $65 billion aimed at getting equity-like returns based primarily on doing collars is beyond nutso because it simply can't be done—more so considering Madoff's performance claims of 10 to 12 percent each year consistently. Remember, the whole premise behind the collar is you can't make or lose much.

But Madoff didn't need to fool everyone—just enough people. A $10 million investor may not want to admit he doesn't understand how split-strike conversions work. When asked, one Madoff investor said "Even knowledgeable people can't really tell you what he's doing. . . . People who have all the trade confirms and statements still can't define it very well."[3]

To my knowledge, there's simply no money manager of any form of any material size who's had any long-term, market-beating success using primarily or even heavily "split-strike conversions" and doing little else. But I've been in this industry 37 years and am battled-scarred and jaundiced by years of observation. How can an Average Joe know if a trading tactic is suspicious? More important, how can you know?

## Like a Hammer to the Head

Easy—always be cynical about flashy-sounding tactics and murky strategies. Collars aren't bad. But they aren't a strategy at all; they're tactics. A tool—neither inherently good or bad. Like a hammer! Hammers are great for nails, not so good for screws, and downright dangerous if someone's coming at you with the claw end aimed at your head. A hammer won't help you eat ice cream. It's all in the application. Used appropriately, fine. Used indiscriminately, bad.

And nothing says "flash" like a good *derivative*. For decades, nay, centuries, investors have sliced, diced, and repackaged risk—and profited from doing so. *Derivatives* are any security whose value *derives* from the price movement of something else—whether it's a stock, bond, commodity, loan, mortgage, you name it. If used properly, well, and when appropriate, derivatives can be very useful. If misused, they can be pricey or even seriously ding returns.

The derivatives most investors run into are *options*—whether puts or calls—and can be on single stocks or even indexes. There are myriad ways to combine options—collars, straddles, butterflies, strangles, iron condors (how's that for mumbo jumbo?), on and on. I needn't detail them all here; you can find straightforward descriptions on any finance website (even on iron condors).

Fancy tactics are just tools—useful in some ways, useless in others, and, at times, potentially dangerous. Appropriate use is fine. Indiscriminate use almost never is.

Beyond options there are endless trading tactics—selling short, going double long, buying futures, forwards, swaps, on and on. Some tactics are just more appropriate for certain investors than others. And certain tactics make more sense under specific market conditions. Most important, indiscriminate use of *any* tactic is a red flag. But so is any strategy description not rooted in sound finance. Another way to say that: If it sounds suspicious, maybe it is. If it sounds like mumbo jumbo, it probably is.

### Derivative Drivel

This is not to say options themselves are bad. They aren't. Honest advisers use them all the time—the same is true for any tool. Rather, be suspicious if the tool is touted as a magical cure-all—able to net outsized returns reliably. The same way you would be suspicious if someone told you they could get you great investment returns because they had a magic hammer.

Claiming to trade complicated sounding derivatives—options, futures, etc.—is a favorite fraudster tactic. Probably this is because cons know they can more easily find victims unfamiliar with how complicated derivatives work—concealing the scam longer. Or maybe they know investors won't fall for the notion of super high and perfectly consistent, too-good-to-be-true returns based on a simple, well-diversified, plain-Jane stock and/or bond portfolio.

Joe Forte, who the SEC charged with bilking $50 million, claimed to trade S&P 500 index futures.[4] Robert Brown, who allegedly embezzled about $20 million starting in 2000, promised he could double investors' money in 8 months through option trading.[5] He also disturbingly claimed he *never lost money* in stocks. I met him once—a local guy. Had a drink with him! I wasn't talking business because it was a social event. He went down that path. When I heard him say in that very short time period—over just one drink—that he never lost money in stocks, it was perfectly obvious I didn't need to and shouldn't have another drink with him. Not to me, but to others, he even promised if any investor lost money with him, he'd pay the difference out of his own pocket.[6] Sound nice? Sure—except such an arrangement, unless from an immediate family member, should always be a stark warning of someone up to no good.

## Getting Short

Kirk Wright—the NFL embezzler—claimed to get big returns by shorting stock.[7] Shorting is a perfectly legitimate tactic—useful at times—if not an overriding portfolio strategy. Let me say that again. Something like shorting is a tactic, not a strategy. A strategy is figuring out based on some form of information when and what to short.

When you *sell short*, you borrow a security (a stock, an index, a bond, etc.) and sell it, hoping it will drop big so you can buy it back at the lower price and repay the lent security. The difference between the price where you sell the borrowed stock and the price where you buy it back is profit (less interest on your borrowing). If you have a valid basis for envisioning a stock or even the entire market will drop big and long, shorting can make sense.

You can get big returns by shorting—but it's risky, like buying single stocks is risky. Just because you sell short doesn't mean the price will drop. You can borrow a stock, sell it, and the stock can easily rise hugely! Then, you must buy the stock back at a *higher* price, taking a loss plus the interest you owe on the borrowing. This happens all the time.

Shorting is another inherently short-term timing game. Stocks tend to rise more than fall over time (revisit Table 2.1), so to make consistently big returns shorting stocks, you must be a super-duper stock picker. And even then you likely wouldn't only short stocks, but short some you see as falling while buying others you see as rising.

History's most legendary investors have all been men who predominantly didn't short. Most have overwhelmingly been long-only buyers. You name the name, and they may have shorted a little from time to time as a tactic, but they weren't just selling short and mostly didn't. I don't know this for sure, but I doubt Peter Lynch ever shorted a stock in his life. Ben Graham, Warren Buffett, John Templeton, Phil Fisher—you name the name, and they were noted for what they bought, not for shorting.

Hedge funds buy long and sell short. Someone like George Soros—legendary, indeed—goes both ways. History's most famous short-only investor as far as I can tell, is Jim Chanos of Kynikos Associates. He's currently very active, 51, in the prime of his career, very bright, been at it a long time, has a great history, and obviously had a stunning 2008. I went against him once a long, long time ago and he cleaned my clock. I respect him. I'd be very skeptical betting against him because he is very good. He is, among other things, famous for shorting Enron early and thoroughly. And he has a long laundry list of trophies where he shorted stocks that then went bankrupt. More power to him. No one I've ever known is as good at picking those as he has been. Yet he has never been on the *Forbes* 400 or *Forbes* Global Billionaire lists, while lots and lots of long-only buyers are. I mention this to point out that the most successful short sellers haven't been as successful financially as the most successful long-only buyers. Why?

My father taught me this when I was 10 years old. When you sell short your upside is limited because stocks can only go to zero. You can only make 100 percent on an un-levered basis. But if you buy the right stock or other asset, you can make much more than 100 percent. So, unless you're Jim Chanos, selling short as your only tactic is basically a loser's game in my view. Thought through another way, since stocks have risen over history a lot more than they've fallen, it just doesn't make sense that selling short gets consistently big positive returns. Take Kirk Wright again. He claimed he did that—consistent, big returns by shorting. Should have been a red flag for anyone since the whole time he operated, up to when he was outed, the market was overall rising. Much tougher to short in a rising market than a falling one for obvious reasons.

## Penny for Your Thoughts

Another popular, mumbo jumbo rat tactic is pushing penny stocks. Penny stocks don't really sell for a penny. Rather, any stock not listed on a major exchange (NYSE, AMEX, NASDAQ, etc.) can be called a penny stock.

Penny stocks aren't bad—they're just typically very, very thinly traded. And they can be difficult for the armchair, daunted investor to follow—which is why some rats love them. It's easy to deceive victims about the value. A rat can't lie about GE's price—you see it every day in newspapers and scrolling on TV. But you must know where and how to look for penny stock info, and cons will target those who won't look (Daunted Daves and Concerned Carls). Famous historic fraudster Walter Tellier used, literally, "boiler-room" sales tactics to push phony penny stocks. He was charged by the SEC in 1957 with swindling about $1 million, but he probably got vastly more. (Read more about Tellier in Appendix C.)

## No Charge

While not a trading tactic, odd fee arrangements can be a bad sign— like Brown's offer to pay back investing losses out of his own pocket. Normal adviser fee arrangements are a percent of your assets they manage. Stock brokers typically charge a commission on the products they sell. That's normal. Advisers tend to offer similar fee structures— whether a fee for service, commissions for products, or a percent of assets under management. If you see something unusual—*like an adviser charging trading costs only*—that could be a bad sign, requiring more investigation. Anything unusual when it comes to fees is a red flag.

Investors universally hate paying fees. Who wouldn't? But put the shoe on the other foot. Would you work for free? Even if you love what you do, your time is worth something. If someone's fees are low—much lower than other comparable managers or alternatives—it's not necessarily the bargain of the century. It's likely too good to be true. First, you generally get what you pay for. Second, no one works for free. That manager could be getting paid to recommend certain products not necessarily in your best interests. Or he could be paid by embezzling. Both bad! Be sure to ask how your adviser is compensated. Make sure it makes sense and isn't unusual.

Madoff didn't charge an adviser fee—he charged only transaction costs.[8] True—Madoff also owned the broker-dealer. Some adviser/broker-dealer dual-registrants might operate that way. But I'd ask, doesn't that give them incentive to trade? If not an embezzler, that could be a conflict of interest. It might make sense strategically to make very few trades in a given year, but if trading is the only way to get paid, advisers might find reasons to trade more.

Being suspicious of Madoff's fee structure might have saved you. Insult to injury, "feeder funds" that directed assets to him generally charged clients 1.5 percent or more on the assets under management. (More on feeder funds in Chapter 5.) Normally, feeder funds would share the fee with the master fund. But because Madoff charged only for trading, they got to keep the fee—potentially very lucrative, particularly when assets seemed to only magically grow.

This was, of course, a red-flag conflict of interest for them because, in choosing to put money with Madoff, they were choosing to put it where they made the most short-term fee. Do you think these feeder funds had additional incentive to direct client assets to him, and not question his tactics too hard? Feeder funds may not have been in cahoots and didn't know he was a scamster, but they should have been more cynical simply because his fee relationship was unusual for their industry. And that's what clients paid them very handsomely for—due diligence. That they weren't cynical is a telling condemnation every one of them will never live down.

## Fool Me Once

There are con artists who'll fool with fancy, perhaps academic-sounding tactics—collars, options, shorts. But they won't just get you with fancy tactics. Sometimes, all an effective con needs is persuasive talk and a murky strategy.

Kirk Wright used this tactic, too. In an official prospectus, he claimed one of his funds "seeks to capitalize volumetrically on a few select opportunities characterized by moderate to high valuations, compelling business fundamentals, and strong management teams."[9]

Volumetrically? And people bought it. If I heard the word "volumetrically" I'd run away with as much volume as I could. Wright's early investors couldn't (no Google back when he started), but a simple search on that term doesn't return anything finance-related. It's nonsense mumbo jumbo. But it appealed to folks with a sucker gene. It had that ring of "consultant-ese." Remember, his victims weren't stupid. But folks who consider themselves smart may not always question—they don't want to reveal they don't understand. Many smart people have a hard time getting their egos to openly admit they don't understand. Forgoing your ego on Wright's strategy could have saved you.

Madoff, too, knew his strategy was murky. If asked directly about it, he claimed it was "complicated" and "proprietary" and he couldn't go into it further.[10] Nonsense! According to some clients, Madoff actually became "testy" if questioned. He didn't even want clients talking with each other—he threatened to ban clients who talked among themselves![11] There's no reason for such behavior unless you're hiding something. Legit managers shouldn't fear extracurricular chatter about their strategies.

## Stamp Strategy

Confusing with flashy tactics and a murky strategy is age-old. Ponzi himself attracted victims by touting an inscrutable strategy. He claimed to arbitrage currency spreads through investing in international postage coupons. Stamps! And this was supposed to yield 50 percent in 90 days. (And I have a bridge to sell you.) As federal agents closed in on him, he defiantly claimed innocence, that he was being victimized because his "proprietary" techniques were so successful! But people fell for it, not because they were witless dupes, but because they didn't reason out if such a return on that asset was even possible.

## Strategy Mumbo Jumbo

Some may say, "But I understand very well how derivatives/options/ shorting/etc. work! I wouldn't be fooled!" Hopefully not! But con artists aren't looking for only the financially illiterate—they're primarily looking for folks who won't investigate or complain—because they're too intimidated, too busy, or otherwise too unsuspecting.

And don't forget—victims were fooled, but they weren't stupid. There were big investors who lost huge amounts with Madoff, and huge institutions, including hedge funds, who were duped. Hedge fund managers know exactly how most option trading strategies work. Yet Tremont Group Holdings as a feeder fund still invested $3.3 billion—more than half what they managed—with Madoff. Ascot Partners invested pretty much all of its $1.8 billion with Madoff.[12] There were a slew of huge banks—HSBC, Holland's Fortis, Royal Bank of Scotland, BNP Paribas— together investing billions.[13] These guys aren't dummies. Yet they too got bamboozled. Why? They didn't investigate closely enough—didn't get the five signs. That's all; that's it.

Some who did investigate the strategy closely walked away easily— probably didn't lose any sleep over forgoing Madoff's supposed big returns. Interestingly, absent from Madoff's victim list are the biggest of the big pension funds—Harvard, Duke, Penn. No state pension funds. NYU lost some money, but they currently have a few lawsuits pending because they "disintermediated" the decision making for part of its funds and didn't realize one of their advisers had hired Madoff.[14] (See Chapter 5 on how disintermediation can trip you up.) Why?

The biggest pension funds and endowments have intensely rigorous vetting procedures. They aren't impressed simply by great returns. Typically, they look for managers who manage to a specific benchmark— just like you should. And they put a lot of effort into fathoming how and why the manager has varied from that benchmark over time. Vast performance deviations from that benchmark not rationally explained and fundamentally supported—like getting positive, consistently similar returns year-in, year-out—knock managers out of the running for their money. (I know this inside out because a big part of my firm's business

is getting hired by these entities.) They don't care if a manager supposedly gets 150 percent every year—*if they can't understand the manager's
strategy pretty darned well, they won't hire the manager.* The same discipline
should be true for you. And, though institutions may hire consultants
to vet managers for them (and usually do), they typically also do their
own rigorous in-house due diligence on top of what their consultants
recommend. They're serious about it. So, get serious.

Rats aren't looking for financial illiterates. They want victims
who won't question too hard—either because they're busy,
intimidated, or easily distracted by outsized performance claims.

One "hedge" fund manager, James Hedges, met Madoff in 1997.
Madoff didn't pass Hedges's sniff-test. Hedges was immediately suspi
cious that Madoff also custodied client money (fraud sign number
one!). Good for him! And good for his clients. But Madoff's strategy description also rankled (fraud sign number three). Hedges asked
Madoff repeatedly to describe the strategy more simply. I don't know
Hedges, but I'm guessing he's no dummy. He could understand complicated trading tactics. But Madoff couldn't describe his strategy beyond
the same mumbo jumbo from the marketing material—the most
Hedges could get was the standard "split-strike conversion" line. Hedges
couldn't see how a bunch of collars should get the performance Madoff
claimed—and that worried him. Because the strategy Madoff described
didn't link to the performance, Hedges walked.[15] Bravo!

Credit Suisse was another bank who saved at least some clients from
Madoff. In 2000, Oswald Grübel, who later became CEO, had a similar
meeting with Madoff and couldn't make sense of Madoff's strategy—
it didn't link to his returns. He recommended clients who had
money with Madoff to consider yanking it. Some did! Others didn't.

(Credit Suisse didn't have discretion over these clients' assets and couldn't force them to sell.) At the time, Credit Suisse clients pulled about $250 million from Madoff. Not everyone listened, though. Between fake returns and clients adding new money, when Madoff was outed, Credit Suisse clients lost about a billion total. But clearly Grübel's recommendation saved some clients.[16]

## The Investment Blueprint

The problem isn't the tactics. Options, futures, forwards, swaps, shorts—they're just tools, neither good nor bad. Sure, they can be used very badly and inappropriately—different issue. The red flag is tactics sold as a strategy. Never mistake a loose collection of tricks and tactics for a strategy. If they are being sold that way, that's a red flag.

Ask an adviser, "What's your strategy?" It's not a hard question. Advisers shouldn't demure. They aren't giving away state secrets. I can understand why a manager won't detail exact portfolio holdings to a non-client—doing so could hurt current clients. But there should never be anything secretive about a *strategy*. You don't give anything away by detailing strategy.

Think of a strategy like a house blueprint—a simple piece of paper that does a lot. The blueprint tells you what the house will generally look like and how big it will be—anyone can see that. It also tells someone skilled at reading blueprints what materials should be used, how long it likely takes to build, and about how much you should pay the contractor. It tells the contractor where to put walls, windows, and plumbing. It's useful during construction and even after! The blueprint sets expectations—for the future homeowner and everyone involved.

A strategy isn't a collection of tools. You may have the world's best band saw and power sander, but without a blueprint, you won't get anything significant built.

Things can go awry. Maybe you can't get the tile you want, so you swap it out. Maybe a monsoon delays building for a while. But the blueprint remains the overall guide. You can't line up a hammer, a screwdriver, and a band saw and tell a contractor, "Now build me the house I want!" So you want your adviser to be able to describe his blueprint so you can understand it.

## Just Three Goals

Fact is, investors sometimes struggle with what's a good strategy because they can't clearly articulate investing goals. The financial services industry can be your enemy here and often ends up confusing investors. For decades, financial product marketing has told investors they're unique and have myriad complex goals—only satisfied with a plethora of unique financial products, sold to you by the industry! And few people argue when they're told they're unique. Fact is, most people aren't so unique. Instead they're individual.

Statistically, unique means you're weird. Way out of the bell curve. Unusual! A couple of standard deviations from normal! Most people are actually very similar to hundreds of thousands of other people in terms of age, investment time horizon, cash flow needs, wealth levels, and other circumstances. They have needs, and those should be met, but very few people are truly unique—just individual. Yet the more you come to believe you're truly unique, the more you come to believe you need a unique financial solution that requires unique product combinations. This is good for financial sales people who will sell all that to you. And the more financial products you buy, the more fees you pay relative to your total net worth. And, all else being equal, the additional fees—upfront and ongoing from a multitude of products with no clear strategy—ding your return over a strategy that's otherwise cheaper and/or more passive.

A strategy should be clear, and so should your goals. Just one of three simple goals fits most all investors.

Another problem: Investors are also taught to think of their assets in disparate pockets. In this pocket, we keep our safe money—for capital preservation. This other pocket is for retirement. This is for growth. That pocket is to buy a vacation home. And in this little pocket is the play money—for taking big gambles. But even if you have multiple accounts—an IRA, a 401(k), taxable accounts, joint accounts with your spouse, a trust, etc.—the right way to think of all your money is holistically—a single portfolio. Because it is!

For sure, that's what finance theory says and says it clearly. Portfolio theory as it exists today derived directly from the revolutionary Nobel Prize winning 1951 writings of Harry Markowitz. He not only redefined how we think of diversification but also, to this point, that you shouldn't think about different pockets of money. Rather, you should think of your entire net worth as one pile. Yet people don't think that way. Never have. Interestingly, the very word "investment" derives from the Latin word "vestment," meaning "clothes." The term was originally derived from *clothes* because you put this money in this pocket and that money in the other pocket and some other money in the third pocket. That's the wrong way to think about it, but that's how we normally do it.

The right way to think about it is as your *overall* portfolio—no matter if it's in 1 account or 12, split into taxable, tax-deferred, trust accounts, etc.; or whether it's managed by one or multiple decision makers. Which means, overall, you should have one easily defined, overall goal. No matter what anyone tells you, 99.9 percent of all long-term investors have one of just three goals. They are:

- Growth. You need your money to grow to leave to heirs, charity, or whomever sometime in the future, or to fund some big purchase—like a second home. Or you need it to grow to cover all or part of your living expenses—now or in the future, maybe in retirement.
- Income. You need your portfolio to cover all or part of your living expenses—now or in the future—and you don't care if there's a dime left. Let the last check bounce, so they say.
- Both. You want your income to stretch to cover living expenses, whether now or later, and you want some growth, too, for the future.

In an overly simple sense, that's it. Growth, income, or both. (There's a fourth possible goal—capital preservation—but despite people frequently thinking they want this, it's actually a rather rare long-term investing goal. Capital preservation means preserving the absolute value of your portfolio through an absence of risk. Without some degree of risk, you don't have growth. You can't even beat inflation without some growth, so we'll set aside capital preservation as a goal. See it this way: If you truly require capital preservation, you probably aren't hiring an adviser so you wouldn't hire an embezzler anyway.)

Envision your goals that way and thinking about a strategy becomes easier. So going back to the con artist rat—ask yourself just why does a "split-strike conversion" help you with long-term growth? It doesn't. How does shorting help with income? It might, at some point, but it's not an end-all strategy for your goal. Your goals should translate to a return expectation, which should link to an overriding strategy. (To read more on goals and how they translate to building a strategy, I direct you to my 2006 book, *The Only Three Questions That Count.*)

## Set Your Expectations

An investing strategy should be clear, easy to explain, and should link to long-term goals. As important, you want to have reasonable, long-term return expectations. This is why you should prefer an adviser who manages to a benchmark—whether it's all stock, all fixed income, or some blend. You can look at what the benchmark has historically done over long periods and make some rational guestimate about what future long-term returns might be. While past performance is no guarantee of future returns, you can at least know if your goal is reasonable. And you can know if the adviser's strategy makes rational sense—or might be a bill of goods.

For example, Jim's neighbor Bob is thinking of hiring a manager who uses the MSCI World Index as his benchmark. Bob wants to average 25 percent a year for the next 20 years. Easily, you know Bob's expectations are off—no stock index has a long-term average return nearly that high. *Nothing* has a long-term average that high. Could stocks go on a terrific tear and do that well for that long? Sure—maybe. I guess anything's possible. But do you want to bet your future on "anything's possible"? No—you want reasonable expectations.

And you also know if Bob's adviser claims average annual returns of 25 percent, something's seriously awry and maybe fishy. What's he doing? Stocks have an annualized average of something like 10 percent in the very long-term past. For someone to do 25 percent a year when stocks are averaging 10 percent means the manager had to take massive bets that worked out. That's fine—maybe he did. But you should know that if future bets don't work, he might be lagging the market by 15 percent. And if you're truly comfortable with that risk, hey, go to it.

But the fact is no one I'm aware of has beaten the market by 15 percent a year over the very long term. No one! To do that by taking big bets and winning is one thing—but even then, those returns are almost certainly going to be volatile because equities themselves are volatile. So Bob needs to see that this manager he's contemplating hiring is either risky or ridiculous. Knowing what is and isn't reasonable helps make the risky or ridiculous clearly visible.

Having reasonable expectations helps set a proper strategy, but also helps you identify and avoid potential financial fraud.

What if an adviser doesn't manage to a benchmark at all? Maybe he just trades jujube futures? He claims great historic returns—seems legit—but there's no jujube futures benchmark to measure against—no history to check. It's hard to know whether he's done a good or bad job, whether it was skill or luck he had, and whether it's reasonable to expect jujube futures to net similar future returns. You're firing blind. He may not be a scamster at all, but a jujube futures strategy, on its own, may not be appropriate for you. As part of an overall strategy? Maybe! On its own, probably not.

In the same way, an adviser might use options, shorting, or other tactics to improve performance relative to the benchmark. Happens all the time! Perfectly normal and fine. But there's no option benchmark. Your adviser may tell you he's the all-time best option manager ever. Maybe he is! But how do you know? And how do you know what's a reasonable range of future possibilities? You don't.

In contrast, an adviser who manages to the all-stock S&P 500 index can tell you, since 1926, there have been 64 20-year rolling periods. In 62 of the 64 periods, stocks have beat bonds—97 percent of the time. Over those periods, stocks have averaged a 926 percent return to bonds' 247 percent return—beating bonds by a wide 3.7-to-1 margin. When bonds did beat stocks, they beat them 346 percent to 244 percent—a 1.4-to-1 margin.[17] That gives you a framework for shaping future possibilities.

If an adviser says, "I do split-strike conversions. I do pretty good," you can't possibly know what's reasonable to expect! This is why Mr. Hedges and Mr. Grübel likely steered clear of Madoff. His strategy seemed fishy, didn't link to his performance, and they had no way of gaming how likely it was his returns could continue. Red flag, red flag, and red flag!

This helps you avoid fraudsters, but it also helps you make better investing decisions. Maybe you find the all-time, best fixed-income adviser. But if your goals are best met with long-term equity averages, the world's best fixed-income-only manager likely can't help you. The tactics should link to the strategy, which links to your long-term goals. And it's better when you understand what to reasonably expect. (Appendix A shows long-term historic performance of stocks versus various fixed income allocations.)

# Further Reading

You wouldn't start firing away with a pneumatic drill before knowing how it works. These books can help you understand how and why to use certain investing tools.

## KNOW YOUR TOOLS

- *Getting Started in Options* by Michael C. Thomsett (Wiley 2007).
- *Option Volatility & Pricing* by Sheldon Natenberg (McGraw-Hill 1994). This one is a bit more technical, so it's not good for rank beginners. But if you want to learn more, start with *Getting Started,* then move to this one.

Don't get sold a murky strategy. These books clearly detail what good pros know about a sound investing strategy.

## NO MORE STRATEGIC MURK

- *The Only Three Questions That Count* by Ken Fisher (Wiley 2006). My 2006 book is based on the straightforward, top-down strategy we use to make investment decisions at my firm.
- *Securities Analysis* by Benjamin Graham (1934). This classic has been re-released multiple times, is still a relevant text, and is in most all pros' libraries today.
- *The Intelligent Investor* by Benjamin Graham (1949).
- *Developing an Investment Philosophy* by Philip A. Fisher (Business Classics 1980).
- *Common Stocks and Uncommon Profits* by Philip A. Fisher (Wiley Investment Classics 2003). Wiley recently re-released my father's 1958 book. Warren Buffett has said he got his value investing from Ben Graham and his growth investing from Phil Fisher.
- *Own the World* by Aaron Anderson (Wiley 2009). This excellent book is an overview on the benefits of global investing.

## CHAPTER RECAP

### Question Your Manager

Don't be shy if a manager's strategy doesn't make sense. Ask for details. Press for a simpler explanation. This won't anger a legit manager. Remember, a manager *wants* your business. If he, she, or it can't take time to patiently explain how they do what they do, or doesn't have a dedicated sales or service team that can do it, you probably aren't important enough to them, and you don't want a manager who doesn't think you're important.

To be sure your adviser isn't selling a mumbo-jumbo strategy:

- Ask them to explain the strategy. You needn't understand every nitty-gritty tactic, but the high-level strategy should be clear.
- If it's not clear—ask again.
- If it's still not clear, get very leery.
- Know what your long-term goals are—growth, income, or both—and make sure the strategy links to them.
- Know your adviser's benchmark, and set your expectations accordingly.
- If the adviser can't or won't clearly explain the strategy, walk away.

Hedges, the hedge fund manager who avoided becoming a Madoff victim, asked Madoff to explain his strategy to him "like he was a first-grader." No matter how complex the tactics, a good manager should be able to distill it that simply. Madoff couldn't, or wouldn't, so Hedges walked. Smart man!

You should walk, too. If the manager can't explain his strategy well, and it sounds like so much mumbo jumbo, look for the exits. It may not mean the manager is a rat. It could mean he doesn't have time for you or doesn't have an adequate service team. Either way, you're better off elsewhere, while remembering that sometimes the return *of* your money is more important than the intended or stated return *on* your money.

# Chapter 4

# Exclusivity, Marble, and Other Things That Don't Matter

How can Jim be sure Trusty Time is as good as they say they are? His Trusty rep takes him on a tour of the building—it's beyond plush. The big banana himself clearly does well and has for years. And he's seemingly very active in both charity and political work! The conference room is adorned with media stories, with pictures of him giving away charitable and political contributions, as well as photos of him with famous politicians—not just from America, but foreign heads of state like Tony Blair. And Jim notices one social picture of the CEO on a yacht, casually hanging out with Harrison Ford. The Trusty rep sees Jim ogling and says, "Mr. Trusty is great friends with Harrison." He's on a first-name basis with Han Solo! How cool is that?

This guy is clearly super-duper long-term success-ful—which in Jim's mind speaks to legitimacy and that Trusty Time can be trusted. And he's a nice guy to boot—gives to charity! If something sinister were afoot, you think he wouldn't link himself to so many politicians who might quickly sniff him out. Jim thinks, "If I were that rich and successful, I bet I'd have friends like Harrison Ford, too. I bet he has a lot more celebrity buddies he hasn't put on the wall. I'll bet he's just modest about it."

The Trusty rep adds, "Sometimes we take clients for cruises on that yacht, which is why we don't let just anyone invest. Each client must be approved by the CEO himself." He adds that, normally, they only accept clients with a million liquid, but they might, just this once, make an exception for Jim. Jim starts to panic. What if he won't be approved? What can he do to make them want him?

It's happening again. Jim's being taken in by financial fraud sign number four: Being impressed by exclusivity, corporate bling, and other things that don't matter.

## Sign #4  Your Adviser Promotes Benefits, Like Exclusivity, That Don't Impact Results.

As authorities closed in on Stanford, he proclaimed his innocence in an ABC News interview. He denied running a Ponzi—that if he were he'd "die and go to hell!" (Which may well happen.) He even became teary (pretty common among white-collar criminal rats). Was it remorse? Did he cry for clients' lives ruined? No—he cried because his assets being frozen meant he was off the *Forbes* global billionaire list.[1]

In our great country, you're innocent until proven guilty. Marvelous thing! Madoff made it easy by pleading guilty, so we may say with impunity: He bilked, embezzled, thieved, and stole. Not so for Stanford. He may plead guilty before this book comes out—who knows! Until then, he only "allegedly" bilked $8 billion. But whether eventually convicted or acquitted—it doesn't look good that clients are, for now, missing about $8 billion and he's weeping over lacking a three-line blurb about his big wealth in a magazine. At best, his priorities are way out of whack. And priorities out of whack don't just make a pathetic interview—they are a very real red flag.

Maybe your adviser is dually registered to both render advice and custody assets, but you think they have good reason for it. And maybe stated performance has been over-the-top stellar. You can't quite understand how they do it—but you know it must be legit because your long-time tennis partner uses them and swears by them. You've shaken your adviser's hand, looked into his calm and confident eyes—and think you'd know if he were a crook.

All bad signs—terrible red flags. But assume you know they're red flags and you've got the red eye all over this. If an adviser were running a scam, they wouldn't waste a bunch of cash building a flashy façade, would they? How can things like extreme exclusivity and an over-the-top posh office be harmful? Maybe it doesn't help, but it can't hurt. Can it? After all, it's his money, his office; why shouldn't he spend it on posh-ness and celebrity? That just calls attention to them, and a con artist wouldn't do that. Right?

### Is It Marbleous, or Not?

All wrong. If these are part of the sales pitch—sold to you somehow as benefits, in any way—be suspicious. It's another red flag all by itself, make no mistake. From them, there's no benefit to you or any other client—and no reason for an adviser to promote exclusivity, social standing, mahogany, marble, pictures with movies stars, political affiliations, etc. What an adviser does in his personal life is his business, but those things don't matter, not one whit—don't lead to better performance or greater efficiency. Ask, "What are they trying to distract me from?" You really don't want an adviser who aims to distract. You want an adviser who aims to be transparent—always.

Now, at the same time, something you don't see as having a direct benefit may be because you don't know the adviser's business that well yet. It's perfectly legitimate to ask, "Why is that picture of Harrison Ford with Mr. Big Banana up on the conference room wall instead of in Mr. Banana's private, personal den? And what does his relationship to Mr. Ford do to benefit me and other clients?" Maybe Mr. Banana's strategy is based on investing in movie deals, and there's actually some validity tied to something Mr. Ford does for his firm. Then that would be fine. And it doesn't hurt to ask, "How does this marble help me?" Because if the marble doesn't help somehow, even if you didn't understand before they explained it, then it really isn't "marbleous," and it contributes to the red flag effect.

## Exclusivity Isn't a Benefit

Mark Twain said he didn't want to be part of a club who'd have him as a member. Groucho Marx took that line to another whole generation with great comic effect. When picking a money manager or financial adviser of any form, it's the opposite. If you're doing the courting and they posture themselves in the role of the courted, ask why? Advisers should court you, not the reverse. What benefit do you get from a money manager who runs his business like an oh-so-exclusive club that supposedly otherwise wouldn't take you? Exclusivity doesn't help you—in every form, it's a red flag.

I understand client minimums. Depending on an adviser's strategy and tactics, there can be amounts below which they're too inefficient to benefit clients. Whether that's $20,000, $500,000, or $10 million, it totally depends on what they do and how. It's very typical for larger advisers to have formal minimums that they've established based on sound economics and economies of scale. And some advisers—mostly hedge funds—only accept *accredited investors* (individuals with incomes over $200,000 or net worths over $1 million). All normal and not alarming. (Though, hedge funds may commingle assets—an arrangement requiring extra scrutiny, per Chapter 1.) So if those minimums are based on real concerns, you don't want advisers to vary them for you.

But exclusivity for exclusivity's sake is just a sales ploy. That someone sells exclusivity doesn't automatically make them a rat—it makes them a red flag. But it is a standard tactic among bunko-artist con men. Why does this ploy work for so many con artists? Amazingly, often in life, if you tell someone they can't have something, they want it doubly more—deceitful at best, dangerous at worst.

Madoff was the king of exclusivity. He claimed he didn't market his services at all—his funds were "closed" to new investors, so it appeared. New investors had to be "introduced" by a trusted source. He even asked investors not to disclose they had funds with him[2]—to perpetuate the exclusive club feeling. Secrecy is the ultimate form of exclusivity. If you're trying to impress the gatekeeper so you can get in, you'll be ultra-sure not to question his tactics too hard—that could cause him to decide against you! So you keep quiet and don't question—which suits a con artist perfectly—and that was probably exactly Madoff's plan from the beginning.

Exclusivity might make sense for a social club, but it doesn't for financial advisers. Be suspicious of claims of "exclusivity" from your money manager.

Madoff's investors had to solicit *him*. Backwards and illogical! Your manager should be motivated by the fees generated from your assets and their long-term recurring nature, generated by doing the right thing for you over the long haul. Your religion, affiliation, name, any other affinity-based categorization has zero to do with that—unless of course you yourself are the Pope, president, a Hollywood celebrity, or something similar. Then maybe they want you for bragging rights. But then, they should be doubly soliciting you, not you them. And if they're using some celebrity for bragging rights in marketing and sales, that's another red flag.

### Moving Minimums

And though Madoff claimed to run an "exclusive" fund, recall his minimums were a moving target.[3] He took money from a range of clients—from the Hollywood glitterati to huge hedge funds and foundations to school teachers and paralegals with $50,000 to invest.[4] He wasn't exclusive about who he bilked. Con men almost never are. The exclusivity claims likely were designed to make victims feel grateful he accepted them. Grateful people don't look gift horses in the mouth. That suits a con artist fine.

What does money management "exclusivity" get you? It doesn't lower fees. There's zero evidence it improves long-term performance and, actually, there is evidence it obfuscates returns or the ability to verify them. Maybe exclusivity is something you want in a country club, if you're into that, but not a money manager. If someone is selling "exclusivity" as a benefit, be careful. It won't help you, and those claims may be a distraction from something more sinister.

## Reputation, Reputation, Reputation

The major players in Shakespeare's *Othello* spend five acts fretting their reputations—one's in question, another's under attack, and a third's worried his isn't good enough. What does it get them? Mayhem, a dead wife, suicide, and imprisonment. They'd have been better off not caring a whit what others said about them. But that doesn't add up to five acts.

A good reputation may be ill got, and a poor reputation might be unfair. Either way, don't be too impressed with a sterling reputation or swayed by name calling—neither tells you anything about what someone actually has done or will do.

"Reputation is an idle and most false imposition; oft got without merit, and lost without deserving."

—Iago, *Othello*, Act II Scene III

Bernie Madoff had a sterling reputation—once, and for a long time. He was former chairman of the NASDAQ stock exchange. Illogically, he fostered a close relationship with the SEC—even sitting on SEC advisory committees![5] His firm, Madoff Investment Securities, was a top-three market maker for both NYSE and NASDAQ securities, handling $1 trillion in trades a year.[6] He was a family man—employed his sons, wife, and extended family in his firm. Nothing wrong with any of that! In fact, it all paints a picture of him as a rather nice, hard-working guy. His story was classic, up-by-the-bootstraps Americana—he built his empire from nothing. But, ultimately, that's what it was—nothing. Overnight, his reputation turned from pillar of society to all-time, world-class miscreant. His reputation didn't protect him or his clients.

R. Allen Stanford also had a great reputation—greatly beloved by his adopted island nation Antigua-Barbuda. They even knighted him! How many guys get knighted? How exclusive is that? You can't get knighted if you're a known bad guy, so people presume a knighted person is a good guy. And he was a repeat member of the *Forbes* 400 and *Forbes* global billionaire lists. His name still adorns college buildings and sports stadiums. And soon it will likely adorn the front of an orange prison jumpsuit.

So don't be too impressed by reputation. It's changeable, isn't measurable, isn't tangible, and is easily influenced by factors having nothing to do with ability. Iago's reputation quote is spot on: Some dishonorable con men will buy good reputations via charity and political donations. On the other hand, where someone has done nothing wrong, a few anonymous disgruntled cranks can easily stir up a reputation-damaging hurricane in the blogosphere—where there's no accountability for lying, snarking, defaming, etc. Happens all the time!

I would never believe things I read on blogs about anyone, ever, good or bad. You have no way to know what's behind them, and often it's nonsense. Actually, more often than not it *is* nonsense! The Internet and its natural feature of anonymity bring out the very worst in a great many people. I've seen people on the Internet very frequently pretending to be who they aren't. I've also seen people on the Internet posting as me. It's scary. Don't ever believe Internet blog postings or comments on articles on even major websites. There isn't integrity there, so don't buy it, either way—whether it's helping the reputation or defaming it. The great reputation isn't as great as you hope it is, and the bad reputation isn't so necessarily deserved. Look for reality instead, which isn't the tarnish of an Internet smear campaign or the gild of social, cultural, and political import.

## Reputation for Sale

Remember Richard Whitney, the 1930s con man? Amazingly, he was president of the New York Stock Exchange when Black Thursday hit in 1929—very reputable—but he later embezzled not only from friends, but also from former NYSE colleagues, too. Who would expect the president of the NYSE to embezzle? But it's a simple fact that he did. It's also a simple fact that Madoff did, having been chairman of NASDAQ. Most who have held these functions have been marvelous human beings. Ditto for the folks who run the SEC! Who would expect a head of the SEC to break the law? But that didn't stop James M. Landis, the second SEC top cop, from spending time in the big house—just like Richard Whitney, and at almost exactly the same time. (You can read more on Richard Whitney and James Landis both in Appendix C.)

There's nothing wrong with a nice reputation. Most of us strive for one, which is why we often fall for the guy with the too-good reputation. But in an adviser, what does that reputation really do for you? It's no guarantee returns are any better or even real (as Madoff's clients discovered). And time spent fostering that good reputation is at best likely better spent focusing on some productive task—managing money—which in the long run will be the final futuristic reputation deciding factor. Today's reputation, here and now, just doesn't matter (except to fools, gossipmongers, snarks, and anonymous Internet posters). Plus, good con artists are beyond skilled at creating an impressive façade. They can easily build what looks like a stellar reputation simply by:

- Making large charitable donations
- Being active politically
- Pandering to affinity groups

And doing it all with Ponzied, embezzled money to get more of the same.

On their own, charitable and political donations, social and cultural activities, and other reputation-enhancing factors are not negating factors. What advisers do in their spare time is up to them. And if they give money to groups you like, that's nice, but it isn't important. But if your manager (or the one you're considering) makes a big deal out of their reputation based on these factors, dig deeper—because none of these things benefit you. If it's not a direct benefit to you, it doesn't make sense to promote it. Digging deeper doesn't hurt—an honest adviser won't mind and fully expects it, and you could end up protecting yourself from financial fraud.

## When Charity's Uncharitable

You may like it when a money manager supports the same charities you do. Charitable giving is wonderful! I personally plan on leaving the bulk of my net worth to Johns Hopkins School of Medicine. My grandfather was in the third graduating class of Hopkins Med (as I wrote about in my 2006 book *The Only Three Questions That Count*), and the institution has always been near to my heart for the vast societal good their research does and will do. But anyone can give to charity if they have spare change. It's not a sign of competence or much of anything else—in money management or anywhere. It isn't a reason to hire me. The decision to hire a money manager should not be predicated on how much someone gives away or to whom.

Case in point: Alberto Vilar (mentioned in Chapter 1) was a famous opera lover—giving *over $300 million* (of mostly his clients' money) to fine arts.[7] His charitable side did not extend to his treatment of clients—he was convicted of fraud in 2008. My guess is most of his clients were not consoled by the fact their missing money was supporting opera globally.[8]

Charitable giving is nice. Everyone should do it, if they want. But it's no reason to hire/not hire an adviser. Charitable giving shouldn't be sold as a benefit to you—it isn't.

"Sir" Stanford gave millions to non-profits, including museums, the Kiwanis Club in Miami, and most prominently, the St. Jude Children's Research Hospital.[9] There's not much further from reproach than helping sick kids—unless your charitable contributions help create an image that helps you rip off clients, as it appears with Stanford.

Madoff was connected to a whole slew of charities. The charity he gave to most was the Lymphoma Research Foundation—over $1 million in 2007. He must have liked them, and there is much there to like. Curiously, this charity *invested nothing* with Madoff.[10] Or perhaps not so odd—a slew of charities who did invest with Madoff have been devastated, including the Jewish Community Foundation of Los Angeles, which lost $18 million; the JEHT foundation that was bankrupted and closed down; and the Elie Wiesel Foundation for Humanity that lost almost all of its assets.[11] Perhaps Madoff knew when his jig was up, he didn't want his favorite charity to be impacted. Not so very charitable!

## Political Pandering

Folks naturally tend to gravitate to like-minded people. If you're a strong Democrat, you may not trust an overt Republican with your money, and vice versa. This is a mistake. First, because partisanship is dangerous in investing—it blinds you to real factors driving markets. Many Republicans think a Republican government is better for stocks, and Democrats believe the reverse. They're both wrong—historically, one party isn't materially better for stocks overall than another, though partisans can and will slice and dice data to support their ideology and see what they want to see. If we look at the history of professional investors, there's no evidence that Democrats or Republicans or folks of neither persuasion do any better—none.

Political leanings are fine. Most people have them, one way or the other. But your adviser's political activity and inclinations shouldn't sway you either. This is akin to the charitable giving—it doesn't take competence to give to political parties or candidates, just some spare change and a preference. Of course, many large firms and money managers cover their bases by giving to both—and then try to get back benefits for their firms from the political process. That doesn't matter to you either.

Political biases are dangerous in investing and not a good reason to hire an adviser. Your portfolio doesn't benefit from an adviser's political connections.

Political alliances just don't matter when it comes to picking an adviser—they don't lead to better investing decisions, returns, or service for you. Still, in democracies, we all have a right to our political views and political activities. So does your potential financial adviser. But just as with charity, if an adviser markets their political life to you, take a closer look at their motivation.

Note, Madoff gave generously—over $1 million in 2006, mostly to the Democratic party and causes.[12] Stanford was more politically agnostic, giving $2.4 million to federal candidates and spending $4.8 million on lobbying since 1999 for both Republicans and Democrats. Amazingly, he lobbied *for* the Financial Services Antifraud Network Act.[13] How's that for irony?

Instead of being confirmation of an adviser's honesty, excessive political involvement could be the reverse—a sign a fraudster knows politicians aren't anxious to bite the hand that feeds them (and feeds them a lot). It just looks off to me when advisers jump in the political fray. First, they have too much to do to stray far from their normal world. Second, it can look like there are ulterior motives that maybe benefit them more than clients. If they're not blinded by bias, they might be trying to distract you from something else.

But make no mistake. Con rats love creating the image of political connectivity, because victims fall for it. The cons know associating with politicians creates the image of them being close to the law, which implies obeying the law. Plus, politicians are a form of celebrity in our society, although it's clear to me that status isn't justified. Still, politicians do have that status, and it rubs off on the rats who can build the connection. It's why they do it. It's why we fall for it. It's why you should see the red flag.

## Affinity Groups

Most folks have one or a few affinity groups—people you self-identify with and have strong connections to. A church, a club, an alumni association, a sporting group, a local community, even extended family. Associations exist just for affinity, like the AARP. Or the Sons of Italy. Or the Daughters of the American Revolution, Native Sons of the Golden West. The list is endless and there's nothing wrong with any of these. I belong to a number of such groups and I encourage you to join whichever groups you care to as well. Like people enjoy fraternizing with like people.

Selling to affinity groups is very common. You've probably been hit up by a young member of a club or an alumni group for something. For young salespeople just starting out—in any field—it can make sense to do this, at least at first. The benefit is these people are likelier to let you in the door and hear you out, even if just from sympathy. It's good practice—even if no one buys. The drawbacks are, if you blow up (which newbies are likelier to do), you can alienate yourself—big time—from people you'd otherwise like to have longer-term social connections with. If word circulates around your group that you're no good, it can move fast, hard, and be long lasting—which could impact your social life with the group.

But for more established salespeople, and particularly extremely capable ones—in advisory work or otherwise—there's no benefit to affinity selling. In fact, there can be a distinct disadvantage. I suppose, if selling cars, you might give a discount to your golf buddies or your alumni group, out of fondness. But what benefit do you get from having a money manager from your affinity group? None at all. If you're a Norwegian-American does it matter that your money adviser is? Of course not.

In fact, affinity selling can be suspicious. Think about it: When you need a dentist, do you want to do research, make a list, check references, and do boring due diligence? No! You ask your buddy, "Who does your teeth?" You've likely done this for doctors, mechanics, pet-sitters—and had very few problems. And if recommended by a trusted person, you may do less background digging. That's probably fine for finding a dentist, but not good when vetting financial advisers aimed at avoiding financial fraud.

Would-be embezzlers know recommendations from an affinity group or even friends generally get far less scrutiny. There's a reason why Utah is sometimes known as the "fraud capital of the world" and has an abundance of "multi-level marketing" schemes (which are another pyramid scam). Utah is predominantly Mormon, and communities are tight-knit—recommendations from friends are simply trusted.[14] Embezzlers know that and plan to take advantage of it.

Madoff used this ploy devastatingly. He marketed heavily to his own Jewish community. Reportedly, an amazing one-third of the Palm Beach Country Club members —predominantly Jewish membership— invested with Madoff.[15] In Madoff's aftermath, the media was shocked that he ripped off his own Jewish community—bankrupting friends, family, charities. But this is what rats do.

Kirk Wright did the same. He won the trust of several former NFL pros and some Atlanta-area anesthesiologists—who in turn sold to their friends and colleagues. Wright's victims trusted him because they trusted their friends and teammates.[16] Dave Dominelli victimized a tight-knit San Diego community. Their affinity groups did not shield them from being victimized. Yours won't either.

It is such a logical "association" for these con men to make in their minds and then in their reality. Because of their affinity, suspicion is reduced. Ponzi himself preyed on his community—Boston Italians— and, as depicted in Chapter 1, they initially revered him! Chanted for him and carried him on their shoulders. It's hard to be the one yelling the Emperor isn't wearing pants when your neighbor, mom, and pastor have him hoisted on their shoulders.

If your golf partner, fellow church member, friend, or grandmother recommends a money manager, don't presume they've done due diligence so you needn't. They may simply and quite innocently be part of the con man's woven web as he spins the web into a Ponzi pyramid.

# Showy Show-Offs

We recently hosted an educational seminar for local clients. Because I own several buildings in San Mateo, California, in which my firm operates, we used our seminar room to keep costs down—in my view, something in my clients' best interests.

We also had tours for clients who wanted to see the buildings and operations. Before the tour, one particular client seemed upset—bristled by something undetermined but obviously annoying to him. But the 2008–2009 market was brutal, so our tour guides logically enough guessed that was the gut issue. As the tour progressed, clients saw our trading operation, where the client services people operate, etc. There's no marble, no granite. It's a nice enough vanilla concrete and glass building, but probably not what most envision when they think about money managers. All open architecture, no one has an office but me— but few begrudge the CEO a door to close. (And it's sliding glass, so they can still see me and I see them.) My employees sit trading-floor style— literally elbow to elbow—because it encourages transparency, but also it's efficient, hence low cost, which keeps fees competitive for clients. Buildings, leases—these things cost money—and in financial advisory, firm costs ultimately are paid for by clients—not quite but almost directly. Why have wasted space when we can make do with less?

By the end of the tour, this client's entire attitude changed 100 percent—he was smiling, seemed relieved. When asked what was behind his transformation, he said he came expecting to see granite, marble, mahogany, and posh private offices. But seeing how we operate made him feel better. That client understood—a fancy office looks nice, but it doesn't make a money manager or financial adviser any better. Warren Buffett has always operated out of modest quarters in Omaha. John Templeton operated out of a lime-green office above a small police station in the Bahamas. Where they are and how fancy their offices are don't matter and don't guarantee your money manager is more competent than anyone else. But the con artist will always go for the fancy office because most investors don't think the way our client did as he toured our facilities. Fancy's not necessarily a negating feature, but it is a red flag.

Showy displays—like a fancy office—that don't accomplish anything for anyone could be a sign a manager isn't as efficient with client fees as he could be, or otherwise has his priorities potentially out of whack. That's not a crime; that's just less optimal for you. If it's over the top, then it could be suspicious. Maybe flashy displays seem harmless. And they can be! A posh office is by no means a sign of embezzlement. But if managers go out of their way to aggrandize themselves and *make a point of that* in their marketing and sales, ask, "Are they gilding the lily with my fees, and why? What are they trying to prove? What is it they want me to think about them?"

In a truly perverse sense, I'd be a lot more comfortable with an adviser who had a super flashy expensive office—but tried to keep clients from seeing it—than one who pushes it at prospects. Optimal is if they don't have a fancy office. Secondarily, if they do, but don't push it as something you should see. After that, if they do push their fancy digs at you, then you need to overcome that red flag issue before moving forward.

## Time-Hogging Hobbies

Beyond corporate flash, other forms of personal aggrandizement—like fancy toys, flashy titles, hobnobbing with celebs—aren't just a distraction, they're an actual negative. Top money men and women don't have much time for fancy toys. To my mind, hobnobbing is the ultimate negative. Clients get nothing out of a money manager who hobnobs. If your money manager displays and promotes photographs of himself or herself with Nancy Pelosi, a president, Bono, or Brad Pitt, be red-flag careful.

To my knowledge, no big-name money manager has ever owned a sports team. They don't have time! They're too busy being focused. Warren Buffett, though not a money manager, is the world's second-wealthiest guy and widely regarded as shrewd and successful—and he doesn't own a sports team. Doesn't have time! He doesn't personally own a jet (though his firm does—he calls it "The Indefensible"—a witticism underscoring his understanding of shareholders' feelings about keeping costs down). He wears schlumpy suits. He doesn't hob-nob. He's too busy managing his long-term successful business. That's a better model for advisers.

My firm advertises a lot. You may know that. We do direct-mail marketing and a lot of direct response Internet advertising. We've done lots of print advertising, radio, and even TV. It's super efficient because folks who respond to the direct marking become prospects who are then called on by our sales force—which converts some of them to clients. It takes relatively little time from senior investment decision makers—hence it doesn't distract.

A lot of people in general and investors in particular, for reasons deeply embedded in our psyche, hate advertising. And they hate money managers who advertise. But it works very efficiently. It's also right out front, in the open, direct, and transparent. The extra clients we get this way bring in revenue, allowing us to do more for all clients—new and old. From that, we've built our research organization and added more and more client service features every year—all paid for by the benefits deriving from our direct marketing (also known as direct response advertising). When people ask our sales people why we do so much advertising, and if that isn't a bad thing instead of a good thing, our people easily explain why it's efficient and benefits our client base. Your question to any adviser should be, "How does all this poshy expenditure benefit me and other clients?" If it does, that's great. If it doesn't, that's a red flag.

If you're in the financial advice world and involved with civic activities more than at the hobby level, it's too much time away from serious work. Again, distraction! If you have time to climb the social ladder, it's too much time. If you have time to be a race car driver, yacht racer, big-time cattle rancher, etc., it's a lot of time. Too much!

I write books on the side. This is my sixth. It takes time. But they're all about what I do work-wise in one way or the other and help me focus on work *while* doing a favorite hobby—writing. I've been writing all my life and am prolific and enjoy it and find it recreational, rather like other people enjoy golf, hiking, sports, etc. For me, writing isn't a distraction—it's a way to recreate while focusing on some part of what my clients and prospective clients are interested in. In my career, I've generated hundreds of *Forbes* columns, dozens of major articles, research papers, and these books.

But each time, I'm forced to sit down and both research a topic a little and commit to what I'm ready to say—that I'm truly willing to have people read now and maybe come back and read decades later (e.g., in this book I've referred you to my 1993 book). But writing has that quality where you commit yourself to what you think is true—to what you'll be proud to have people read even a long time from now. That's good. Helps my clients, helps me, helps you I hope. And I don't have any problem explaining any of this to anyone. Neither do my firm's sales people. So if you're worried about a money manager or financial adviser with a seeming distraction, make a point to ask about it. An honest, straight-up adviser won't be upset by questions and should easily and comfortably answer them in a way that makes sense to you. If they can't or won't, it's a brighter red flag.

Fancy offices, expensive toys, and corporate and personal bling are a red flag. If they aren't meant to distract you, at the very least they distract the adviser.

## Fake Façades and Purloined Pedigrees

If you're ushered into a posh office as part of your sales pitch, remember Stanford. "Sir" Stanford, according to former investors, had spectacular corporate offices. Prospective clients got treated to fine dining by the on-staff chef, who reportedly made a very fine crème brulee—the best one former investor ever had.[17] Turned out to be super-expensive egg pudding.

Sir Stanford personally and through his firm sponsored a slew of sporting events—cricket, golf, tennis, polo, sailing. He also sponsored pro golfer Vijay Singh (who's likely on the horn with his agent now finding new backing). Lots of firms host sporting events. Nothing wrong with that if that's how they choose to spend marketing dollars. Event marketing is a normal tactic many use. But how Stanford presented himself and his firm to the world seemed aimed at creating the flashy façade that suckers fall for.

His office and websites featured pictures of Grandpa Stanford as "founder" of Sir Stanford's financial empire. Stanford himself has stated his grandfather started the business in midst the Great Depression and cited a 76-year history.[18] But it's fiction! Grandpa Stanford, one-time barber, did start a small insurance brokerage firm—Stanford Financial—but sold to a larger firm. There's no linkage between that firm and Stanford's today. Why lie about that? Because false lineage creates the image of commitment, deep roots, solidarity—all things an insecure investor is likely to find comforting. And they are comforting if real. But a rat knows how to make them up out of whole cloth to distract you from seeing what he really is.

Sir Stanford also boldly claimed to be a relative of Leland Stanford, one-time California governor and founder of Stanford University. Very blue blood. But there's simply no evidence supporting that and university officials flat-out deny the familial link.[19] Yet another unsupported claim, designed to make him seem what he's not and make investors not suspect him. Most investors just won't believe someone will simply and out of whole cloth make up something like that. And most won't, but cons will regularly.

Convicted embezzler Alberto Vilar similarly claimed to be from a wealthy Cuban family whose wealth was confiscated by Castro during the revolution, and as a boy they all fled to America, starting out as poor immigrants. It's a great rat tale because it creates the image he's from successful and wealthy genes (and we tend to believe the offspring of the successful are more likely to be successful than the offspring of the unsuccessful—for the same reason a foal of a prize race horse is worth infinitely more than then the foal of a nag). But at the same time, it invokes sympathy for his poor, immigrant roots in the classic American tradition—overcoming a tough childhood to become a super-successful, self-made man. Vilar got the best of both worlds in this image—all-American dream concepts linked to basic sympathy for his plight. Poor him! And great him! It would, however, be a much greater story if it wasn't totally fact-free.[20] I knew him a little a long time ago as he was building his business (and wrote about his villainy in my 2008 book, *The Ten Roads to Riches*). What I said then was that all his stories were just too much—too much red flag. He didn't actually come from Cuba. He came from New Jersey. Not nearly so enticing! His story from the beginning was built on phony baloney. All rat tales are.

Successful offspring of successful people are a real part of our land-scape. There is some sense of pedigree that goes with it in our world, for some reason. That said, I'm the son of a successful person and I've been successful in my career. I'm a direct recipient of that pedigree benefit. I'm very proud of my deceased father's career. I hope you're proud of your father and mother too.

Not making too many comparisons, but there is a very long list of people who are offspring of exceptionally successful people and have been beyond exceptionally successful themselves. The list is too long to waste time on, but a few classic examples include: John Quincy Adams, Warren Buffett, Michael Douglas, Angelina Jolie, John F. Kennedy—thousands and thousands. And that fact makes us associate a form of exclusivity, near nobility, and celebrity to successful people's offspring. So, not always but often, con artists may claim that connection somehow. Because you just wouldn't expect the son or daughter of a famously suc-cessful person to be a rat. But to build the pedigree out of whole cloth, the con artist goes further. He tries to institutionalize a solid image. Stanford, of course, had himself knighted by Antigua—a designation, in reality, which is worth about the prize in a Cracker Jack box.

Creepily, Sir Stanford's staff, from cricket club groundskeepers to traders, all wore gold Stanford insignia pins—a golden eagle—worth, dollar-wise, much more than the Cracker Jack prize. Long service meant a diamond was added to the pin.[21] In March 2009 (two months after the Stanford news first hit), his website only peripherally mentioned

Stanford Financial Group being controlled by a receiver. For you *Lost* fans, visiting that website is Dharma Initiative surreal. Even the wickets in the cricket pictures say "Stanford." Dharma! Yet the website still featured pictures of "founder" Grandpa Stanford and his gold eagle logo—which frankly looks more like 1930s fascist propaganda than the blessed and traditional all-American, genuine Cracker Jack prize so many millions have coveted as children.

Bad branding decisions are not a negating factor. And neither is building a firm culture and creating a sense of community. That's all fine and a pretty normal part of business. But a carefully crafted façade is a blood-red flag—particularly when it's built on lies. There can be no benefit to clients from having staff wear expensive gold and diamond pins, having tiered fountains in the lobby, promoting myths about the firm's founding, or advertising one's position in the Order of the British Empire. (Elton John's been knighted—but at least he was knighted by the Queen of England. Still, do you want him managing your money?)

All else being equal, if you're picking between two advisers with similar strategies and performance profiles, you should naturally want the manager who obsesses less about bling. At the very least, your management fees will likely be better spent. But you also could be avoiding a rat who's hiding something behind a finagled-façade rat tale.

# Further Reading

Whether pulling a financial Ponzi scheme or any type of fraud, con artists tend to use the same basic tactics. Learn how con artists play their victims so you don't fall prey. These books detail not only financial fraudster ploys, but the many tactics con artists use.

### BEAT 'EM AT THEIR OWN GAME

- *The Art of the Steal: How to Protect Yourself and Your Business from Fraud, America's #1 Crime* by Frank Abagnale (Broadway 2002). A good book about avoiding fraud overall from one who knows. It takes a chicken thief to catch a chicken thief.

- *How to Become a Professional Con Artist* by Dennis M. Marlock (Paladin Press 2001).
- *Players: Con Men, Hustlers, Gamblers, and Scam Artists* by Geno Zanetti (Running Press 2002).
- *How to Cheat at Everything: A Con Man Reveals the Secrets of the Esoteric Trade of Cheating, Scams, and Hustles* by Simon Lovell (Running Press 2006).
- *Crimes of Persuasion: Schemes, Scams, Frauds* by Les Henderson (Coyote Ridge Publishing 2003).

## CHAPTER RECAP

## Bothersome Bling

How your adviser chooses to spend his, her, its money and free time is up to them. Don't negate them because they enjoy something you don't or spend money you wouldn't. But if corporate and/or personal bling is used to sell you, be suspicious. Exclusivity, charity, political connections— none of these benefit you, ever. If they are sold that way, that's a real red flag.

Many advisers have nice offices and operate normally. If its over-the-top, you may wonder if they could spend your fees more efficiently, but it's not automatically a sign of embezzlement. But if you're being fed caviar and crème brulee instead of being given straight answers about the investing strategy, enjoy the meal—then find a safer place for your money. Also:

- Be wary of claims of exclusivity. Account minimums are fine and normal, as long as they're applied equally and consistently. But exclusivity in no way benefits you and may only be a sales ploy. Fear being allowed "in" at amounts far below a firm's stated minimum. A rat may count on you being grateful—and distracted.
- Don't rest on adviser reputation alone. Madoff and Stanford had stellar reputations and were widely and universally respected. This didn't help them or clients. And some great managers may have unfairly evolved poor reputations.
- Don't fall into the trap of thinking an adviser who shares your political leanings is better. Political bias can blind, leading to worse performance. And political connections can signal ulterior motives that benefit the adviser, not you.
- Don't give a member of an affinity group a free pass. Subject them to the same due diligence you would anyone else.
- In general, don't be swayed by things that don't matter. Your financial adviser may have a long, interesting history—and that's fine—but that's no reason to hire him, and no reason not to conduct full due diligence.

# Chapter 5

# Due Diligence Is Your Job, No One Else's

Jim's seen enough. Now he must decide whether to hire Trusty Time. He struck out with Big Time—that was close. How can he be sure he doesn't hire another embezzler? The Trusty Time rep walks Jim to the door and says, "I can see you're hesitating. You know, we are registered with the SEC, unlike that Big Time fraud." Jim nods, "That's true!"

But he's still nervous and not exactly sure what to look for. This is an important decision. The Trusty rep gives him a client list—clients who've agreed to let their names be used as referrals. Jim recognizes some of them—one he's played golf with. Smart guy—a surgeon! Jim calls him. Dr. Smarty raves about Trusty Time. Best decision he's ever made—he's been happy for years. Jim thinks Dr. Smarty surely wouldn't hire a fraud—he's too smart!

Jim's about to fall for the fifth sign of financial fraud—he's letting someone in between him and the adviser.

# Sign #5    You Didn't Do Your Own Due Diligence, But a Trusted Intermediary Did.

In the wake of the Madoff and Stanford swindles, the media and politicians asked why were regulators seemingly asleep at the wheel? Shouldn't they have stopped them? When these things happen, people want to point fingers and assign blame.

For some heads-up investors, Madoff and Stanford, though massive and seemingly having long-term steadiness, just seemed off. They walked away. Yet others, for many years, stood by them loyally and sung their praises as clients. The same is true for the smaller recent scams and all scams through history. Some near-miss victims easily walked and lived to tell the tale, while others eagerly signed up. What happened? Are the victims witless dupes? Destined to be duped again? No! Remember—fooled, but not stupid, or even fools.

No—you, yourself, and no one else must do due diligence before handing over any sum of money. Check the guy out! And maybe victims thought they did check out the rats enough. Except, often, victims let someone or something get in the way of their due diligence—an intermediator, a friend, even the SEC. For them, if someone else signed off—like a financial auditor—they thought they needn't look closely themselves Or maybe they didn't realize someone else's due diligence wasn't as rigorous as it ought to be, or that the SEC isn't some form of social insurance against fraud. Or that the auditor might not have audited the reality of the returns, but instead simply the financial condition of the firm.

And for many victims who used and paid intermediaries—like feeder fund clients—they surely expected a higher level of due diligence from a professional and were sadly disappointed. What they didn't realize is, no matter who you hire, who you trust, and how many congressional mandates a body has, due diligence is your job—no one else's. Someone else may not know why it's vital to check for separate decision making and custody, vet if performance is real, check if the strategy makes rational sense, ignore flashy facades and other things that don't matter, and perform the rest of this book's prescriptions. It's not complicated, but enough folks won't do the check—and con artists count on that. It's your money—you and you alone must do the check. Don't let anyone in the middle.

## Helping Those Who Help Themselves

Was it a massive SEC failure that let Madoff function so long? A regulatory loophole? No! Madoff didn't run a Ponzi scheme because regulators forgot to tell him not to. What he did is and has been illegal—forever. In some ways this is no different than hard core drugs—illegal, but some people do it. The near-term benefits for the criminal at the time seem to outweigh the longer-term risks. Laws and regulations don't eliminate bad behavior. Maybe they deter some—but determined villains find a way. Regulators in general and the SEC in particular have taken a lot of flak for not having gotten all these bad guys earlier. I actually have sympathy for the regulators.

If a con artist can fool someone out of a few billion, they're likely skilled enough to fool the SEC too—at least for awhile. And regulators might not have had cause to look into the fraudsters rigorously—because they lacked jurisdiction or the scamster knew how to look legit. After all, Stanford was operating as an Antiguan bank—that's not the SEC's normal beat.

That regulators didn't catch these swindlers earlier is a pretty good indication that you can't count on them to protect you. Only *you* can protect you.

America's regulatory bodies aren't perfect. They can't be. They do their best, but there are overlapping areas, conflicting mandates, fuzzy jurisdictions. Some firms have multiple federal and state regulators, while other firms maybe answer to one state body—all depending on what they chiefly do and sell and how big they are. Too many regulatory cooks mean things can slip through cracks. Even when regulators catch someone they never get credit for it. The SEC did catch Stanford. Exposed him! Went after him! Yet they're blamed for not catching him earlier, when fewer folks would have been hurt. The SEC can't get a break no matter what they do.

Yes, it'd be nice if regulators guaranteed safety, but the truth is, as Ben Franklin said, "God helps those who help themselves." (If you're not a god person, insert whatever power you like.) Though headlines periodically bemoan lack of oversight or too much "deregulation," the finance world is one of the most strenuously regulated spheres in the universe and has been for decades. And my guess is it only gets more regulated from here—forever. But regulation has never stopped frauds and never will (we'll cover why in Chapter 6). Swindlers run right

---

### Regulating Regulators

A separate book could and should be written on whether regulatory bodies should be streamlined and how, and whether that'd be good or bad. But that's not the purpose of this book. For advisers, it isn't our obligation to fuss whether regulation is optimal—it's to adhere to the highest letter *and* spirit of the law because, ultimately, it's better for clients.

For example, as the CEO of a large investment management firm, if I lobby Congress to change regulation to make it the way I think it should be, they'll naturally think I'm only doing it to make it better for me and not better for you, the investor. And then Congress will put me through the wringer. Individual advisers, large or small, have very little incentive to get into this fray. But to my way of thinking, the regulators themselves have a tough job and receive little appreciation.

around rules and are good at creating false illusions that engender trust that lets suckers get swindled.

## A Lot of Transparency Never Hurt Anyone

Not letting anything in the middle of your due diligence means having as few hurdles as possible. You want to see everything—warts and all. Seek adviser transparency and a standard of disclosure leading to heavy regulatory oversight. By and large, this means a firm registered with the SEC.

Non-registered advisers—and there are many—don't have to register with the SEC because they qualify under various exemptions (or can't because they're too small). Which means they may be state registered, and state regulation is generally not as onerous as SEC regulation. If someone manages hedge funds only, he may not register himself or his fund at all! Not with the state and not with the SEC! And that can be perfectly legal, depending on the state. (And of course, some would-be embezzlers don't bother at all, because if you know you're breaking the law, why bother with nit-picky details? Daren Palmer is one alleged con artist who has been charged with, among other things, dispensing investment advice without proper registration.)[1]

That doesn't mean state-registered or unregistered advisers don't disclose material information. Many do! But they don't have as high a standard they must adhere to. Hire them if you must, but doing due diligence on an SEC-registered firm is just plain easier. And an SEC-registered firm is on the SEC's radar and scheduled for routine, surprise inspections. Firms that aren't registered with the SEC still must adhere to state and applicable federal laws, but the fact is they just aren't regulated nearly as rigorously as an SEC-registered adviser.

There are legitimate reasons some firms aren't registered with the SEC—like hedge fund managers or smaller firms—just as there can be reasons for them to be dually registered as an investment adviser and a broker-dealer (which goes against my Chapter 1 rule about separating decision making and custody). In my mind, registering with the SEC just keeps life simpler for clients, all the way around. It demonstrates advisers are aware of client concerns, want to be as transparent as possible, and are perfectly willing to subject themselves to whatever scrutiny their regulator demands.

While there are perfectly legit reasons an honest adviser who doesn't have to register won't, a con artist might not because the registration process could expose them. State- and SEC-registered advisers both must fill out and update regularly an SEC Form ADV—disclosing material information about "advisory affiliates," including owners, officers, and employees. Executive officers and portfolio managers must also disclose their past, their education, etc. The ADV also details things like compensation and custody (Part 9—always check it). That form is the basis of the first inspection the SEC Division of Investment Management does on a typical adviser—potentially exposing the con artist. The ADV does not ask, "Are you a con artist? Do you swear?" But it does provide additional info, making your due diligence easier.

An SEC registration is a good start in deterring some would-be fraudsters—though not foolproof. Still, the registration and the Form ADV are additional tools helping you help yourself.

The ADV also asks whether any "advisory affiliate" (including certain owners, employees, and officers) has been charged with a felony in the past 10 years or a securities crime ever. The SEC won't reject a registration, out of hand, if an owner or executive has committed a crime—though they might! They want to know so they can look deeper. And they want to be sure clients are aware—which is why filings are fully public.

By registering with the SEC, an investment adviser commits itself to reporting and disclosure standards, and marketing and advertising guidelines. Again, the SEC can investigate any time it wants—wholly unannounced—just show up at your door and stay for a week or two. When they do inspections, they have broad powers to inspect your client files, trading records, financial accounting—pretty much anything they want. They're very routine and businesslike about it, but when they make information requests, it's the adviser's obligation to provide them what they've asked for in a reasonable time. Rats may shy away from registering with the SEC to avoid this kind of transparency and unannounced but routine inspections. Of course, a rat can simply lie on the ADV, knowing that the SEC can't fact check all filings. Folks have lied before, and as long as they don't stir up trouble again, the SEC may never find out. That's a dangerous game to play, though, as the SEC won't take that lightly. Big fines and jail time are typical for big SEC transgressions.

But if someone's willing to embezzle billions, they might also not be very precise in their SEC filings—which can actually help you, if you're careful. Example: Sir Stanford registered his firm—you can see his filing online! But he wasn't listed as a direct owner, executive officer, or as someone who directs investments on the Form ADV Schedule A. When I checked, he was listed as indirect owner on Schedule B.

As a client (or potential client), why do you care about A versus B? Because, according to Jim Davis, Stanford's former CFO, Mr. Stanford *was* directing investments and telling him exactly what to state as investment returns. (Mr. Stanford points the finger back at Davis, and courts will have to unwind their disagreement.)[2] If Davis is right, and Stanford was directing investments or his marketing claimed he was, that must be appropriately disclosed on Schedule A. Now, it could be someone forgot to update the Form ADV, and that's not a hanging offense. Still, that would be a discrepancy that, as a potential client, should give you pause.

That pause might lead you to dig deeper. Then, it wouldn't be very hard to discover Stanford had pled a past personal bankruptcy. The bankruptcy was caused, apparently, when a string of small fitness centers failed.[3] There's nothing wrong with failure! Failing, admitting to it, learning, and moving on and up is the American way. Running a small business is tough—they fail all the time. No shame in that. Folks who haven't failed big haven't done anything long enough to be worth listening to, and I'm confident most rational folks won't hold a bankruptcy like that against someone. Especially if they evolved to be successful. Even Sam Walton of Wal-Mart went under once earlier in his career.

However, it's suspicious when folks in this business aren't as transparent as possible. Maybe Stanford knew more transparency might have led investors to pretty easily discover more odd discrepancies, like his tall tale about Grandpa Stanford founding the business, which is promoted in his marketing and on his website.[4] If you'd known Stanford pled bankruptcy, you'd wonder why he was playing around with fitness centers when he was supposed to be running the family business. From there, you might discover Stanford was teaching scuba diving in 1985 in Aruba when he and a European ex-pat cooked up the idea of opening an offshore bank. Stanford got seed money from his father and opened the bank in early 1986.[5] Nothing wrong with that! But it's directly contradictory to his marketing about his firm's founding. A fake history is beyond suspicious. Most cons fabricate parts of their life evolution to make it sound more viable for luring in suckers. And you might have dug this up had you been suspicious about the Form ADV.

If firms commit to transparency, it's easier for you to fact check. And it allows you to spot weird inconsistencies that, if followed, can be red flags saving you.

## SEC, not CSI

At least Stanford registered his firm with the SEC. Madoff didn't register his as an RIA until 2006—didn't have to as a hedge fund manager in New York. My rule about sticking to firms that are SEC-registered would have saved you from Madoff—at least until 2006. Said another way: It would have saved you completely for 18 out of the 20 years he did his Ponzi—which is a good start for one simple rule.

Though the SEC is your friend in transparency, it is not now, never was, and likely never will be a real crime-fighting unit. The SEC enforces securities laws, demands firms disclose all material information that might interest investors, and whacks violators. But it can't possibly spend its limited money and manpower investigating every registrant. There are just too many, and it is and always will be stretched too thin. Don't expect the SEC to do your due diligence for you. SEC registration—though helpful to you—is not, in itself, protection against embezzlers.

Typically, as stated earlier, the SEC rarely finds fraud ahead of time. Just the way it is. The Stanford case was unusual in that they were investigating for three years before the scam became public.[6] The investigation—done with the FBI—was stymied because assets were allegedly held in Antigua. Usually, the SEC arrives after the embezzlement is uncovered or very late in the game—far too late to save most victims. By then, the money's long gone.

Fortunately, in 2009, the SEC announced some changes that might help prevent or at least stymie some larger cons. Now, while routinely reviewing certain "high-risk profile" RIAs, they'll contact clients directly. This decision specifically impacts dually registered firms, i.e., RIAs also registered as broker-dealers. The SEC knows this cold! They know, as per Chapter 1, that the big risk is when the decision maker has custody, and they are now moving that to the front burner of their inspections, and that's a good thing.

Some advisers are complaining—claiming contacting clients only spooks them.[7] In my mind, only those hiding something should complain. If you've done nothing wrong, you'll pass any SEC inspection with flying colors. The folks at the SEC wear long pants—they know what they're looking for. They won't hold it against an RIA if clients are upset or concerned about market volatility, disappointing returns, or if the market didn't go the way the adviser thought it would—all really routine social outcomes that aren't indicative of swindling. That's what the market does—has for centuries. Rather, the SEC will look specifically for securities violations. They'll be rooting out returns that are truly "too good to be true." And they'll zero in on asset value discrepancies—which they can do more easily talking directly to clients.

And for them that's a great step—100 percent justified—but still not 100 percent foolproof. Even if the SEC increases staff 10-fold, my guess is there will still be more than enough villains discovering ways to bamboozle.

## True Crime

I don't think it's reasonable to expect the SEC to catch most rats and certainly not early on. Actually catching and convicting criminals of all forms has always been tougher than most people can possibly envision. Let me take you on a side jaunt to see how tough the SEC's job is if you expect them to protect you from rats.

A little-known fact is that a small percentage of criminals commit most of the crimes. According to Heritage Foundation research, among violent criminals, 65 percent were rearrested for a felony or misdemeanor within three years. According to a study by the RAND Corporation, the average former state inmate committed between 187 and 290 crimes per year, excluding drug deals. That's a whoppingly big number. According to the Bureau of Justice Statistics, over 80 percent of state inmates have at least one previous conviction and criminal sentence, over 60 percent have two, and almost half have three.

Law enforcement knows who these people are and still can't stop them before they've committed lots of crimes and done lots of damage. But with embezzler rats, we don't know who they are in advance. And they're smarter and financially much more incentivized. So I don't think it's reasonable to have high hopes that the SEC will be able to do what normal law enforcement can't do.

Another very scary statistic: When we look at rape, robbery, aggravated assault, burglary, larceny/theft, and motor vehicle theft—category by category—the actual percent of reported crimes that result in any prison time only varied by category from a low of 0.3 percent for motor vehicle theft to a high of 6.7 percent for larceny/theft. The rest are in between somewhere. Those are very low numbers and ones law enforcement doesn't really want you to see. If those were all four times higher, we would still think they were very scarily low.

Now think this through. Does law enforcement catch the smarter criminals or the stupider ones more often? Naturally, they catch the stupid ones more often. Hence, among the smarter ones, the percent of prison time done is even lower. One chief of police told me, "We catch the stupid ones and the ones that mess up because they're on drugs. But the smart ones, we have a very tough time there. Not just catching them but also convicting them. They know the system and they know how to game it." So if police, whose business it is to be out on the street, can't catch, convict, and incarcerate criminals before they've done lots of damage, and the police already know who most of the bad apples are, how could we reasonably expect the SEC or any other government regulator to catch these embezzler rats before they've caused massive mayhem? Plus, these rats are smart criminals, not the stupid and drug-crazed ones law enforcement is best at catching.

Source: National Center for Policy Analysis, Crime in the United States, Uniform Crime Reports, Policy Report No. 149, p 7.

## Blind Spots

There will always be blind spots. We now know Madoff stirred enough suspicion that the SEC did periodically investigate—even before he registered in 2006. Most famously, a bookish accountant, Harry Markopolos, tried to computer-model Madoff's "split-strike conversion" and, even assuming perfect execution, couldn't simulate Madoff's steady returns. In 2000, Markopolos started sending memos to the SEC, one entitled "The World's Largest Hedge Fund Is a Fraud."[8] Damning, but the SEC didn't investigate.

Finally, in 2005, based on his and other complaints, the SEC investigated. Why so long? Who knows—likely understaffed and over-worked and of the view that other RIAs seemed more problematic. Also, the SEC is used to seeing complaints that don't lead to anything. A simple fact that most people don't know is that most complaints don't lead to anything.

Keep in mind, most advisers have had a few complaints. Folks complain about RIAs all the time—not for securities violations but because they're unhappy about performance or fees. There was a lot of attention about the few who complained about Madoff—but, like Markopolos, they weren't clients. And almost every material-sized manager has a few of what I consider bogus complaints in its file sent by competitors, disgruntled former employees, or the adviser's next-door neighbor who doesn't like him—hoping the SEC might find something bad. So the SEC is used to complaints being wrong, bogus, simply disgruntled or what-have-you, and not leading anywhere. The SEC is largely desensitized to it, and they take these complaints, file them, and look into them routinely when they do their next normal inspection. It doesn't usually motivate them to go out of their way to elevate some manager to the top of their radar, because it would elevate everyone to the top of their radar! It's tough to wade through all that to get to actual securities violations.

When the SEC called, they discovered Madoff might have misled that he was registered when he wasn't. So he registered! The matter was dropped, and no enforcement was recommended nor action taken—and he continued his con for another two years.[9] You simply can't expect the SEC will stop all evil-doers before they do their evil-doing. You can help the SEC by helping yourself.

## Feeding the Beast

What if you hand over due diligence to someone you believe should be a pro at it? No matter who helps you make decisions, you're still never excused from doing your own due diligence. Prior to 2009, most investors probably never heard of "feeder funds"—but Madoff's scam made them a household word. It appears that as much as half of Madoff's victims came through feeder funds—and they may never have known they were invested with Madoff until the feeder fund manager called their clients to say the money was gone.[10]

What's a feeder fund? It's not technically a thing—it's just a fund that invests all or part of its funds in another fund. They set themselves up as the "master" fund, commingle client assets, and dole out slices of portfolio management to other advisers. Sometimes called a "fund of funds"—it's a tactic used by registered and unregistered advisers alike. Why? Maybe they commingle assets to get access to institutional advisers otherwise closed to smaller investors. Maybe the feeder fund is located offshore and gets some purported tax advantage. Lots of reasons advisers do this—none of them very useful to you in my view.

A registered "fund of funds" will generally be more transparent than an unregistered one—you can see what advisers they invest in. And they will typically (though not always) invest in other registered advisers. This is ok, but funds of funds are generally costly. Your fee covers not only your adviser's fee, but also the fees of the advisers it hires. This is much less efficient (and much more costly) than buying directly. Directly is always cheaper. Plus, there's no evidence funds of funds perform better than single funds. None! In fact, if nothing else, higher fees mean you're almost guaranteed to lag. And just because your adviser checks out, it doesn't mean the advisers it hires won't raise red flags.

Think of it this way. The feeder fund you put money into charges you 2 percent annually plus 20 percent of the profits—a typical feeder fund arrangement. It puts the money in 20 funds that charge it 2 percent annually, plus 20 percent of the profits. Of those 20 funds, some do better and some do worse, but probably the 20 overall don't do much better than average. But before you get anything, after all costs, you're giving away 4 percent plus 40 percent of profits. What's the likelihood you're getting really good returns? Not so high.

A feeder fund adviser might check out ok, but you may not know who it hires on your behalf. Layer upon layer of obscurity! You want transparency.

Like advisers, feeder funds can be unregistered. They set up as a hedge fund and dole out funds where they choose. (They don't call themselves feeder funds, by the way. They just say they're seeking good investments on your behalf.) Now you're really in someone else's hands. Maybe they invest with another adviser who's not registered. Or you get a feeder fund who invests in another feeder fund. Layer upon layer of obscurity! And it's all legal—just not particularly rock-solid safe.

Many Madoff investors had no idea they were even invested with Madoff, because their feeder fund invested for them. The most basic due diligence wasn't possible. Beyond risky. Plus, investors in feeder funds have virtually no recourse if something goes awry. You're probably not covered by standard SIPC insurance you get with a non-connected broker-dealer. No FDIC, of course, which covers bank deposits.

Let's say you did due diligence, checked out Madoff, and didn't like him—whatever reason—so you hired someone else. If that adviser was a feeder fund, you could have still ended up invested with Madoff. It happened to so many investors. Fairfield Greenwich Advisors—a Connecticut-based hedge fund—lost about $7.5 billion to Madoff—half the assets they managed.[11] Tremont Group Holdings, one of the most famous feeder funds based in Rye, New York, lost $3.3 billion—more than half their assets. Luxembourg-based Access International Advisor's had one fund—LuxAlpha—that invested 95 percent of its assets with Madoff—all gone.[12] It's beyond amazing that anyone would invest in a feeder fund without knowing where their money was going.

One might assume a feeder fund or fund of funds diversifies among managers. And many do. But some funds were 100 percent invested solely in Madoff. That's a tough phone call for an adviser to make, but it's infinitely tougher for the client—you. In these cases, the intermediary— the feeder fund—got in the way of good due diligence. You don't want that.

## Intermediator in the Middle

Fairfield Greenwich is now itself dealing with a fraud charge from the state of Massachusetts. Authorities charge Fairfield Greenwich failed as a fiduciary and didn't fulfill its claims of rigorous due diligence.[13] Maybe, maybe not. Up to the courts. And there may be more charges against feeder funds as victims demand more heads roll.

A good rule of thumb: Never pay a big fee to someone to get in between you and the ultimate decision maker. Many advisers use intermediaries to sell their products—broker-dealers like Schwab, Merrill Lynch, Smith Barney, etc. Maybe those RIAs don't have in-house sales people, or they do and just want more sales channels. Selling is fine! Part of the advisory business—if you're in the RIA business and you don't have clients, you don't have fees, and you don't have a business, so you aren't really in the RIA business. Selling just comes with the turf.

Never pay a big fee to someone to stand between you and your ultimate decision maker.

Some broker-dealers have programs where, for a percent of your assets annually, you pick from a stable of RIAs to manage different portfolio slices. These RIAs usually focus on a particular size or style—large cap growth, small cap value, emerging markets, or whatever. The broker sells you, the prospective client, on the benefit of having access to advisers who normally have high minimums—maybe out of your reach—but as a client of the broker-dealer you get in the door with less. Plus, the broker-dealer tells you they've vetted the RIA choices for you, making sure you get good ones—improving the quality of your results while making it easier for you. Sounds great, but this puts an intermediary in between you and the advisor again. That's a no-no.

Don't accept someone else's legwork—you should still fully vet the ultimate decision maker. You don't really know what kind of due diligence they've done. The fee you pay to a feeder fund or broker is technically just a finder's fee—sometimes a steep one. And if you think your broker-dealer or feeder fund adviser will avoid all potential evil-doers, just remember Fairfield Greenwich.

These relationships have other problems that aren't about embezzlement at all. The advisers you hire through your broker don't talk to each other—so one may be selling a stock another's buying. No net change in position, yet you've paid two transaction fees! Plus, what made the one sell and the other buy? Are their strategies at odds? You don't know, because you can't talk to the adviser—your broker is in between you and the guy or gal actually making decisions. Or they all may be piling into the same things at the same time. You think you have diversification among them because you have five different advisers, but in reality there's potentially much less diversification than you thought—maybe none. If you do use someone to help you find an adviser, make sure after you hire them, there's no one and nothing in between you and the decision maker and you're not paying an ongoing fee to the "finder."

Many large institutions like state and corporate pension plans use institutional consultants to find advisers and help in vetting. But what they do is very different from what most all individuals can do. Institutions typically demand and sign off on a rigorous course of due diligence the consultant must follow. Their due diligence can take years to conduct and produce stacks of documents. This is normal and has served institutions well—like those from Chapter 3 who steered clear of Madoff because his strategy didn't make sense. Meanwhile, these institutions routinely do their own due diligence on top of what their institutional consultants do—just as you should do your own—to make sure, in a belts-and-suspenders basis, they don't get hoodwinked.

Most individuals just can't do the intense due diligence an institution can—they don't have the time or staff. But you can learn from what they do—do your own leg work and don't be swayed by "too good" performance or other things that don't matter.

## Unfriendly Friends

Friends are great, but no matter how deep your friendship, or how much you think they know about business or investing, a recommendation from friends is not due diligence. As shown in Chapter 4, con artists know folks are likely to trust referrals from friends and are very good at working that angle.

While fine for finding a mechanic or pet sitter, this is a grave mistake when it comes to investing. Madoff had a number of "unofficial" agents who acted as his intermediaries—clients who liked Madoff, trusted him, and touted him to friends—and in some cases received compensation for the referrals.[14] Referrals are fine! It isn't illegal to get referrals, nor is it illegal to pay for them. However, it is illegal to pay for referrals and not disclose it to the new client. But do you think that would stop Madoff? And the clients doing the referral certainly didn't know the law requires the referral fees to be disclosed.

Friends make nice dinner companions and give a good shoulder to cry on. But a tip from a friend—no matter how smart or sophisticated that friend—is never sufficient due diligence. Friends don't let friends in the middle.

Richard Spring acted as an "unofficial" agent connecting Madoff with victims—from multi-millionaires to school teachers with relative pennies. He lost $11 million himself—almost all he had.[15] Carl Shapiro, a known philanthropist, invested much of his net worth and almost all his charitable foundation money—$500 million. And his son-in-law, Robert Jaffe, also invested heavily. They too, unwittingly, led more friends and family to Madoff.[16] They obviously meant no harm! They just believed in the returns they got, and because they believed, their friends believed. Friends make bad intermediaries.

Professional organizations will also sometimes have advisers they recommend. This is how many of Kirk Wright's victims found him—the NFL vetted him and added him to their list of "trusted" advisers.[17] Taking the recommendation at face value hurt. Without independent due diligence, victims couldn't see he commingled assets, reported wildly unbelievable performance, had a murky strategy, claimed tactics that didn't link to the returns he reported, and promoted a flashy façade. All classic red flags you missed if you relied on someone else.

## The Myth of the Tiny Auditor

The SEC, a professional intermediary, a friendly referral—none are rock-solid protections against fraud. And neither is a professional audit—not necessarily—but not for the reasons many think. Many early news stories whacked Madoff and Stanford for using small,

## Sex Is Good—The Sixth Sign of Financial Fraud

I'm going to say something new, then contradict myself. There's a sixth sign of financial fraud. It's an easy one—one that hasn't been said in public (to my knowledge) and is politically incorrect. It's perfect—almost 100 percent accurate in history—though I'll refute it looking forward.

To perfectly avoid big-time embezzlement ratsoes historically, you could have simply never hired any male adviser. If you've gotten this far and haven't noticed that every single big-time rat mentioned is male, you should think about your ability to observe and learn fast from patterns. And if so, then you should be really, really careful about focusing on the return of your money more than the return on your money.

Of course, with all due respect to the feminine half of human-ity, none of history's legendary investors, with the exception of Hetty Green, have been female—and few females would willingly be Hetty Green. (If you don't know Hetty, she's quite a character. Find more on Hetty in Appendix C.) I'll bet there were many women who knew Hetty Green and wondered if she really was female—despite having birthed a son.

And the fact that essentially all of history's legendary investors have been male has set up a sociological precedent—a form of cover, if you will—for all con artist rats to be male. It's harder for us to envision a female as a great market guru, when none that we've known of historically ever have been. Con artists know that and play on it—hence male. Women trying to be Madoff would have a harder time pulling it off. The too-good-to-be-true returns would pop out as too good to be true. And the female rat attempting the scam would get so much media attention and personal scrutiny she would likely be outed soon.

It's not that there have been zero female rats. It's just, overwhelm-ingly, they've been male. The only historic female rat of any mate-riality I can identify was Boston's Sarah Howe. In the 1880s, she ran a ladies-only fund, promising 8 percent returns, and got away with about half a million. Like all rats, she targeted her community and had direct access to the till. Then there's the very recent case of Clelia Flores, charged with running a $23 million Ponzi targeting her own Los Angeles Hispanic community. And there's Stanford's right-hand, Laura Pendergest-Holt, charged with obstruction. Was she party to the (alleged) fraud? Up to the courts. But even if found to be in cahoots, she still wasn't head rat, and in that regard she seems the perfect exception that proves the rule. With all the intense focus on Ponzi schemes in 2009, if there were more big-time female rats, you'd think they'd have surfaced. But instead, all you get is the usual parade of male rats.

Hiring a female in history to handle your money may not have gotten you Warren Buffett or Peter Lynch, but it surely avoided Madoff or Stanford. That said, women are equally as crafty as men and fully as able to discern how to maneuver the rat's maze of embezzlement. And there are plenty of women in prison for other forms of dishonesty from petty theft to burglary to working in the accounting department at a naïve firm and embezzling from the employer. (For which there is also a simple solution but outside the scope of this book. See Appendix B for how to avoid this form of rat.)

But there may very well be future lady rats! One theory I have is that so much attention will have been focused on Madoff, Stanford et al., that some crafty women will see an opportunity. It wasn't that long ago that there were no female heads of state or corporate CEOs. Now they're increasingly common and will be more so in the future. Similarly, there will be more opportunities for a female rat to embezzle, particularly because women are traditionally seen as more trustworthy—tying back to their historical roles in positions like motherhood, teachers, nurses, etc. Hence, if a female rat postures herself right, she ought to be able to gain people's trust and overcome all the five signs of financial fraud and become a Sheford or Madwoman rat, pretty easily.

A second and sad theory of mine is that, while most will read this book with the intent of avoiding the next Madoff, something like 2 percent will read it hoping to figure out how to embezzle more efficiently. How, in effect, to game the five signs. And some of those 2 percent are apt to be female. The unintended consequence is this is a basic textbook for wanna-be embezzlement-based rats. Rats are everywhere and there's no reason men should have a monopoly on future rodent results. So I'll bet within our lifetime we'll see more women rats pulling off financial embezzlement.

Source: *Associated Press*, "SoCal Woman Accused of Running Ponzi Scheme," *BusinessWeek* (April 13, 2009); Evan Perez and Kara Scannell, "Top Stanford Official Is Arrested," *Wall Street Journal* (February 27, 2009).

no-name auditors. It was easy for folks to poke fun at the auditing firms, described as "tiny," "three-man shops," and "dingy." Some described the measly square footage of the offices or the back-water towns they were in.

But a small auditing firm isn't a negating factor. Why? We don't know what those "small" auditing firms were auditing! Auditing firms audit any number of things. Just because someone contracts an auditor doesn't mean that particular auditor is vetting performance or the assets. It will come out in the legal process, but for now, it appears, at least in Madoff's case, the auditor wasn't contracted to audit performance but, rather, financial solvency.[18]

Auditing financial solvency is a perfectly normal and standard function for auditing firms. So shouldn't their small size automatically be a red flag? Still no. Because even a big-firm financial audit isn't rock-solid protection against fraud. Keep in mind, Enron used a then-Big Five auditor—Arthur Andersen. In the process of Enron's bankruptcy, Arthur Andersen itself got taken down, so the Big Five are now just the Big Four. Enron just fooled them! A HUGE firm! (The remaining Big Four accounting firms are PriceWaterhouseCoopers, Deloitte Touche Tohmatsu, Ernest & Young, and KPMG.)

AIG and Lehman both had their financials audited by a big outfit just before they went kaput. LuxAlpha, the hedge fund that invested 95 percent with Madoff, was audited by Ernst & Young and checked out fine.[19] Ivan Kreuger (the Match King) was audited by Ernst & Ernst—a monster, high-quality, big-name firm back then (predecessor to Ernest & Young)—and they found nothing wrong.[20] For that matter, as 2008 evolved and big banks had gonzo writedowns of trillions of dollars they all, every single one, had a Big Four auditor.

Today, the Big Four are a form of oligopoly—as, by the way, are the big credit ratings agencies Moody's, S&P, and Fitch's. There's no real competition between them—there never is when an entire industry is spread between three or four vendors. It isn't in their interest to engage in real competition. In a social policy sense in this time of financial turmoil, one of the things we haven't quite learned as a society is that competition is good. A form of protection and one of the things the government should do is break up the auditors and rating agencies into at least 10 players so they begin actually competing with each other. Having just three or four doesn't lead to effective service.

I'd never fault any firm—any industry—for using a non-Big Four firm. In all fairness, if you're a public stock, dependent on bank loans, or dependent on the rating agencies, you're pretty much required to use a Big Four auditor—but only out of tradition. But that doesn't make it particularly beneficial. If, for example, we were a private firm of some size and wanted to raise a debt offering through a major investment bank like Goldman Sachs, they would require that our financials be audited by a Big Four firm. And investment bankers usually require a Big Four auditor to do a public stock offering—because it looks better on the surface. Or if we wanted a bank to put together a large syndicated loan for us, the bank would require our financials be audited by a Big Four firm. But if we don't need any of that, there isn't really any advantage to a Big Four auditor and a lot of costs and nuisance. There are plenty of perfectly fine regional accounting firms capable of doing audits. But if any form of asset manager specifically touts getting a clean bill of health from a Big Four auditor as a positive to you, that should ring suspicious. (Enron touted Arthur Andersen's review to the public the whole way down the drain.)

Conversely, don't assume a no-name auditor is a red flag. Most folks, and probably you, can't name any audit firms outside the Big Four anyway, unless they or you are an accountant. So even a decent size regional firm might sound "small" when it isn't. Even a smaller firm—I have nothing against small business. You can't get big if you don't start small—a small accounting firm might offer great service for a great price. That's true in everything. There are plenty of honorable CPAs working for themselves or small offices. I can't fault a smaller-scale money manager for keeping costs down (which ultimately benefits clients by keeping fees lower) by hiring a smaller outfit. And remember, they may be auditing the financial solvency of the firm, not its investment returns.

As for performance auditors—all the more reason why GIPS performance reporting standards (as covered in Chapter 2) are another useful tool for you in determining if an adviser is legit, because GIPS standards are globally consistent. In my view, con artists wouldn't want to report using GIPS because it's just too much consistency and transparency. Bad for them; great for you.

# Further Reading

Doing your own due diligence is just easier with the SEC as a partner. These books give you good historic context of how and why our current regulatory structures evolved.

### HELP THEM HELP YOU

- *Abuse on Wall Street: Conflicts of Interest in the Securities Markets* by the Twentieth Century Fund Steering Committee on Conflicts of Interest in the Securities Markets (Quorom Books 1980). You'll have to find this book used, but it's worth it. This is a good historic take on the kinds of client-harming conflicts regulators must grapple with.
- *The Transformation of Wall Street: A History of the Securities and Exchange Commission and Modern Corporate Finance* by Joel Seligman (Aspen Publishers 2003).

## CHAPTER RECAP

### Shortcuts Can Cut You

It's tempting to look for shortcuts—including when hiring someone to manage your money. But by relying on friends, politicians, the SEC, or others to sign off on an adviser, you open yourself to risk. Don't let anyone in between you and the ultimate decision maker. And be sure you:

- Demand an adviser who has rigorous standards of transparency. For the most part, SEC-registered firms will be simpler for you to vet.
  - But an SEC registration alone isn't any form of safety guarantee! The SEC isn't a crime-fighting unit. They set and enforce rules and punish transgressors. It's rare for them to uncover fraud ahead of time. Help them help you by doing due diligence.
- Check the Form ADV—both parts! Look for inconsistencies, like a figurehead not listed as a chief executive or owner.
  - Remember, con artists may just lie on public filings.
  - You want the ADV to generally jibe with what you read in marketing materials and what your salesperson tells you.
  - Also, if there is some disclosure they don't want you to see, they're going to put it in the ADV, not in their marketing material.
- Avoid "feeder" funds and other funds of funds. Besides increasing obscurity, these can layer on additional fees that, all else being equal, dampen performance.
- Never accept a recommendation from a friend or associate at face value. Not even from a family member! They might not have done the due diligence you need. Only you can.

Some advisers may help you rat themselves out simply with their attitude about the SEC. Madoff reportedly got nervous when the SEC called, insisting employees wear their "best suits."[21] No reason to get nervous or put on a show for the SEC unless you're up to something. It's just normal in this business for the SEC to look into your firm periodically. The SEC looking isn't a red flag—getting bent about it is. You want a firm that welcomes the SEC with open arms, is open about it with clients, and shows no fear.

Also, ask if they manage money for institutions. This isn't fail-safe, because Madoff and Stanford both managed money for some large institutions—*but almost no state pension funds or major corporate pension plans.* These plans have beyond rigorous due diligence standards. If the adviser checks out with lots of state and corporate pension funds, they're more likely to pass your due diligence, too. But you still must do your own due diligence. And for a recap of exactly what to look for, and why, no matter what, there will always be more villains—read on.

# Chapter 6

# A Financial Fraud–Free Future

Markets were rough in 2008 into 2009. But unless you truly believe capitalism is done, you know stocks will recover not only from this bear, but from every future bear. (And if you don't believe in capitalism and believe stocks will only ever tank, forever, you may need a different kind of book or a therapist.)

Fact is: Every bear market is followed by a bull; we just don't know the exact shape, nature, and timing of that evolution. Sometimes they're faster, slower, bigger, more erratic—and those are all issues that can be and are debated at every turn. But humanity makes progress, science makes new discoveries, human capital grows, and all that gets reflected in future bull markets. So if your assets haven't been carted off by a rat, you get to enjoy the next bull market to some degree.

Even if you don't understand the fundamental reasons why stocks should net superior returns over other asset classes moving forward, most folks do rationally grasp that they can't stash cash under a mattress if they don't want to be ravaged by inflation. And so, forever, some folks will want advice on how to get better than mattress-like returns— whether in stocks, bonds, commodities, or whatever. And there will always be people, for better or worse, trying varied ways to get those higher returns while offering services based thereupon to the world. And, interspersed among them, rats will forever find ways to embezzle.

But simply: If you watch for the five signs of financial fraud, you can avoid having your money Madoff with. **The first sign is simply the most vital.** If the decision maker doesn't have custody, and assets aren't commingled, the other signs, while still important, are less dire. If you're set up right, where the decision maker doesn't have custody, he/she/it also can't boast of too-good-to-be-true returns. Can't—because you can see for yourself exactly what your assets are doing. You don't rely on them to tell you what your money's doing. You can see for yourself, 24/7—you have full transparency.

If your adviser doesn't have custody, they can still have a murky strategy or use flashy tactics ineffectually. But no matter how goofy the strategy or tactics, if the adviser can't get to the money, you know they aren't using them to create a false front for fake performance while carting money out the back door. A goofy strategy may not be so optimal for your future, but I'd much rather have a goofy but honest adviser than a really smart rat.

And your adviser can have the world's most ostentatious office. Maybe he spends his spare time (and some working hours, too) obsessing over charity work with Bono and yacht races. And maybe he's got Nancy Pelosi on speed dial. Again—that's less optimal for you, but at least you know he's not trying to pull a disappearing act with your money.

And if your adviser can't put his paws on your money and cart it out the back door—well, you could still pay 100 people to get between you and them, racking up huge and money-losing fees to intermediators, which would be silly. But as long as neither the decision maker nor any of the 100 intermediators has custody, your money is safe—if not particularly well-managed.

And as long as no one's Madoff with your money, you still have assets and a fighting chance for the future because you can get rid of a goofy but honest adviser and replace him with a better one, or fire all those intermediaries and manage your money better. But you're still living under the principle that sometimes the return *of* your money is more important than the return *on* your money.

## Takes a Pirate to Catch a Pirate

As the scam post-mortems are done and brought to light, suddenly it seems quite obvious to everyone that the rats were always rats—the benefit of 20/20 hindsight. (Folks always do this after a major event—say, "Of course I knew when no one else did. I saw it coming from a mile away!" Were that true, many, many more people would have spoken up earlier, and ultimately fewer people would have gotten hurt.) But people don't really foresee these things, whether they later fool themselves into thinking they did or not. And, yes, there are always thousands of signs and hundreds of missed opportunities that, theoretically, could have been foreseen to have stopped them—if not before they went rogue, at least before too many were hurt. But usually all of us are so busy, focused on what we focus on in life, that we don't see those signs and missed opportunities in our peripheral vision.

Folks groan now that the SEC didn't move sooner on Harry Markopolos's warning about Madoff, or on complaints from at least five Stanford employees starting in 2003 that it was nothing but a Ponzi scheme.[1] But playing woulda-coulda-shoulda doesn't help you protect yourself and actually doesn't help anything at all.

The SEC is mandated by Congress to oversee advisers, regulate securities issuances, and generally make sure investors have appropriate material information about securities. If anyone could or should stop the rats before too many are victimized—theoretically it should be them. Right? But no matter how many process improvements they make, they'll never stop 100 percent of future Ponzi rat scams. Why?

Well, one reason is because they'll never hire pirates.

To outrun pirates, hire a pirate. Queen Elizabeth I knew this vital rule when she hired Sir Francis Drake to lead her navy. Drake was a pirate—bedeviled the Spanish for years—before turning legit at Elizabeth's request. (Though the Spaniards never saw him as anything but a pirate.) She knew she could get her navy men to follow a pirate— it's in a navy man's nature to respect authority, even if that authority used to be a pirate. But a pirate would never, ever follow a navy man. Letting Drake lead her navy was pure genius tactically—ending the reign of the Spanish Armada in 1588 in one fell swoop.

But putting a pirate in charge is a tricky thing to do. Pirates swagger. They swear. They enjoy looting, pillaging, and raping; then boasting about it. They like to say things like, "Arg, matey." I have no idea why, but they do. But you can count on a pirate acting in ways a naval officer wouldn't care for—behavior that is anathema to an admiral. A naval officer respects order, pedigree, and rank. He isn't boastful; he's disciplined. He doesn't pillage; he serves.

Madoff, Stanford, and the other rats are pirate-like, but they've learned to pose as navy men. They rape, loot, and pillage, but they do it all while pretending to be sophisticated, cultivated, and civilized. The flashy façades, charitable work, and political connections all fool victims into thinking they're dealing with a member of the Queen's navy, when really they're being boarded by a pirate.

## The SEC as the Queen's Navy

The SEC in some ways is a little like the Queen's navy. Both are bureaucracies. Both have rules to follow. Both have a hierarchy. For example, a normal path for high-ranking SEC officers is going to a top school, then law school, focusing on securities law—rather like going to the Naval Academy. Then, they graduate and go work at the SEC or the Fed or some other regulatory body. And that's not so different, either. But once they distinguish themselves at the SEC, they leave for private practice—usually securities law or investment advisory work. But the naval officer doesn't leave the navy.

While in private practice, they're specializing in some legal area that derives from the laws that set up our current investment system— usually referred to simply as the 1933 Act, 1934 Act, and the two 1940 Acts. (If you're really in the know, you refer to them collectively as "the Acts.") They start as a low-level beginner in private practice—if they were in the navy they'd be swabbing decks or working in the kitchen. They work their way up, then leave and head back to the SEC once again (or the Fed or . . . or . . . or . . .).

After another stint with the SEC, it's back to private practice again— this time at a higher level, doing more securities law. Someone who's done well both at the SEC and in private practice at a high level and has been politically active and seen as trustworthy and ethical gets picked to be SEC commissioner (one of five) or another top spot. It's often broken down by party. The commission's five spots can't have more than three of one party. So Democrat presidents pick Dems for the commission, if they can, up to the three maximum. And if they have to pick an opposition party member, they try to get opposition-light folks. Republicans obviously do just the reverse. But all very regimented, pedigreed, respectful, and naval. If you serve well, you can be picked to lead.

The real difference with our navy analogy is officers don't go in and out of the navy. But private practice law work not only pays infinitely better than government work, it also exposes practitioners to the ins and outs of the other side of the table, which adds valuable perspective to the SEC's work and isn't easy to get otherwise.

Still another path is simply being career SEC—like being a career naval officer. Career SEC folks usually don't become commissioners, but they still might fill high-ranking spots. Whichever path—these are folks who are seen as good, solid, never cross a line, never rape or pillage. Not pirate-like at all.

And that's why they'll never catch a Madoff or Stanford early on. They don't have a crook's mindset. That way of thinking is unfathomable to them. Because they'd never do what Madoff did, they can't fully imagine how they'd do it to catch these people very early on. Mind you, if you wanted to catch a pirate early on, you would have to go down to the wharf, hang around in pirate pubs, associate where pirates do, and be with them. But a naval officer is never going to hang out in the pirate pubs and say, "Arg, matey." Just no way. And, ironically, this is the exact opposite of how the SEC was initially set up. When the SEC was established in 1933, FDR didn't pick a navy man at all—he appointed Joe Kennedy to head the commission.

## Chicken Thieves in the SEC

The Democrats still went nuts when FDR appointed Kennedy—though a lifelong Democrat, Kennedy was to them an embarrassment! In Kennedy's life, he contributed to his massive fortune by manipulating Wall Street—he was a master manipulator and proud of it. He boasted of it, like a pirate! He famously told a friend, "It's easy to make money in this market. We'd better get in before they pass a law against it." He'd regularly use his influence to hype a stock—advertise it by trading it, he called it. When folks flooded to his stock, he'd start shorting it as it fell back to a more reasonable valuation. Did it all the time!

And, like a pirate, he had miserable ethics by almost anyone's standards. For example, he had been holed up for seven weeks in a suite at the Waldorf-Astoria, interspersing manipulation of Yellow Cab stock with drunken binges with one of his many mistresses, when by his own admission he realized that he had forgotten his wife must have given birth to their child by then. Having not seen his wife Rose the whole time, he sobered up, shut up his hotel suite, bid the mistress away, and went to meet his newly born daughter Pat—by then fully a month old. Pat wouldn't have noticed the absence of her father. One presumes Rose was pretty self-sufficient, but she must have had a pretty clear idea who her husband was, too. And this drink-addled binge, of course, was while Prohibition was in full swing. Not that he ever let Prohibition stop him from getting boatloads of Scotch into the country—sealing his image as a bootlegger. He was a known bad boy and not politically correct. He also increasingly over time wanted social respect, which led him to court and contribute to FDR's presidential campaign. Many say it was this desire for respectability that motivated him to push his sons into politics.

But when FDR actually appointed Joe, enemies in his own party claimed it was merely payback for Joe's hefty financial support of FDR's campaign—and maybe it was, at least to some extent. But FDR thought about this more the way the Queen thought about Sir Francis Drake. When asked about Kennedy, he said openly that "it takes a chicken thief to catch a chicken thief"—implying that Joe was a chicken thief, to put it mildly. FDR further stated that he was the right man for the job because "he knows all the tricks of the trade."

FDR made Joe promise to stay out of the market, and he did, getting to work outlawing most of the methods he had used to manipulate markets. He knew what to look for—he just thought through what he would do and got lawyers to write laws against it. We owe most of our modern securities laws to that original chicken thief. And in his stint as the very first SEC Chairman, he got very high marks for his accomplishments and how he conducted himself. So much so that it became the basis for allowing FDR to later make him ambassador to Britain—always a prized, plum assignment. (For more on Joe Kennedy, chicken thief, turn to Appendix C.)

And that's how the SEC could catch more evil-doers earlier. Other industries have done it. In the early days of the Internet, if a firm got hacked, some of them hired the hacker to set up their Internet security. And Frank Abagnale Jr., after whom the movie *Catch Me If You Can* (starring Leonardo DiCaprio and Tom Hanks) was loosely based, was a check-kiting con man who, after a stint in prison, turned legit and started his own security consulting firm—sometimes working for the FBI. If the SEC wanted to get truly serious about stopping fraud earlier, they wouldn't lock up Madoff and Stanford (if convicted). They'd hire them plus the ghost of Charles Ponzi. They could hire one of the lesser rats—but they probably wouldn't be as imaginative as Madoff. Those three would think through what they've done and would do and create the basis to write laws against it.

But folks everywhere would be outraged, and should be— rats who steal $65 billion shouldn't be rewarded with a government pension. Congress folk would be outraged. The papers would be outraged—which is why it really can't be done and won't happen. But it is also why the SEC will never ultimately be as good as it could be at catching the bad guys early enough. It takes a chicken thief to catch a chicken thief. FDR knew that, but only FDR could pull it off. It's hard for a navy man to imagine a crook's crooked mindset. So, since you can't count on the SEC protecting you from rats, you have to do it yourself.

## Due Diligence Checklist

You've mastered the signs and now know, no matter what façade or psychological ploys scamsters use, they all have the same, predictable rat format.

Of course, as said before, not everyone who uses this format is a rat. Some advisers choose to dually register and take custody of assets, and some choose to commingle assets. Many make use of options and other more advanced trading tactics. And some certainly have luxurious offices. Rats know this and mimic, as best they can, a legit operation so they can avoid detection long enough to bilk enough victims. You can best them by avoiding any set-up that gives a rat or would-be rat the opportunity to evolve to rattiness.

And to avoid the rat, the following is a recap—a brief checklist of questions to ask and things to look for to ensure the adviser you hire isn't now or won't become a rat.

## Separate Decision Maker and Custodian

First and foremost, you want to **separate decision maker and custody**—this is the number one, most important step in avoiding a rat. Make sure you:

- Ask the adviser or decision maker who has custody.
- Check Item 9 on the Form ADV. (Find it online at www.adviserinfo.sec.gov.)
- Make sure the custodian is a large, well-known, deep-pocketed institution with 24/7 Internet access.
- Make sure assets will be held in a separate account, in your name. You don't want your assets commingled.

If you decide to hire a dually registered firm—a firm that's both an RIA and a broker-dealer—know there's additional inherent risk. Make sure a rock-solid wall exists between the decision maker and your assets and the firm has protections in place for you.

If you hire an adviser who commingles assets—like a hedge fund— that's your choice, but you're taking yet another layer of risk and must do additional, rigorous due diligence. Then, you really want a firm that's SEC-registered. Performing due diligence on a firm that's registered with the SEC is just easier on you.

Remember, for years, investors looked in Madoff's eyes, shook his hand, and thought they knew him and could trust him. He gave to charity and politics generously and was, by all accounts, known as a pillar of society. He fooled his closest friends and even, it appears, his sons. Without a rock-solid separation between decision maker and custody, it's very hard to know who's honest and who's an incredibly talented pirate rat in navy clothing.

## Remember "Too Good to Be True" Usually Is

Madoff and Stanford and other smaller rats operated for years with impunity because no one complained—returns were so good! Great performance claims lure victims in and, once netted, keep them docile. But great returns aren't so great when they're fake. Know what's reasonable to expect. If an adviser's returns seem too good to be true, know maybe they are—no—probably they are.

- Ask what your manager's benchmark is, and check what that benchmark has done historically.
- Ask the adviser to show you a bad year. Bad years are fine—everyone has them—and they show legitimacy and integrity.
- Ask the adviser to explain performance discrepancies from their benchmark. The explanation should link to their overall strategy and be rooted in sound finance.
- Know that *no manager with a record close to or beating long-term equity averages will be positive every year.* Getting market-like returns means having market-like volatility.
- Be suspicious of consistently positive returns, or similar annual returns, year-in, year-out.
- Be very suspicious of performance that wildly beats long-term equity averages.
- Know your market history. Average returns aren't normal; normal returns are extreme.

If you want consistently positive returns, you can aim for that, but only if you accept much lower long-term average returns. High returns with consistency are unlikely and a huge red flag.

## Don't Be Fooled by Flashy Tactics

Rats don't want just the financially illiterate. They also want smart folks who aren't too likely to question. The easy way to do that is to simply intimidate—with mumbo-jumbo talk about a murky strategy or a string of confusing tactics. There are some smart folks whose smart-person egos don't like admitting they don't understand, and they make the best rat victims. To not be like them, make sure to:

- Understand what your investing goals are—and know they should be very straightforward.
- Have reasonable expectations based on sound finance.
- Demand a thorough, straightforward explanation of the investing strategy—one that's easy for you to understand.
- Make sure the adviser's strategy links to its performance claims.
- Question the adviser, hard, if the strategy isn't clear or if the tactics don't make sense.
- Know that, while a manager probably won't want to detail precise holdings if you're not a client, *they aren't giving away state secrets by divulging their strategy.* They may want to stay mum on specific tactics until you are a client, but they can and should give a very clear, concise description of their strategy.

If the adviser can't or won't describe the strategy to your satisfaction, walk away. It's a sign they either can't describe it well, don't have time for you, or are up to something more sinister. Either way, you don't want any part of that.

## Ignore Exclusivity, Marble, and Other Things That Don't Count

A fancy office is fine and a plush waiting room is comfortable. And if your adviser's active in charity work, that's nice. But know there are some things that impact you, and many things that don't—and an adviser's personal and corporate bling, social connections, and political contributions just don't help you. In fact, they can be a distraction to the adviser. At the very worst, if promoted heavily, that could be a red flag a rat is trying to distract you from his nibbling.

To understand if a flashy façade's pure flash or a potential smokescreen:

- Ignore claims of exclusivity. You don't want a manager who claims to be exclusive because it doesn't help you. Investing minimums are fine and normal, as long as the manager sticks to them firmly. If you're well below the firm minimum, and the manager lets you in "just this one time," take your money and run.
- Don't rely on reputation alone. Neither a good nor bad reputation may actually be warranted. A good reputation is easily bought, and a bad reputation may be the work of a few illogical cranks.
- Disregard charitable, political, and social connections—none make an adviser more skilled or more efficient. Charity's nice, but a skilled con knows some victims will believe a "nice guy" won't embezzle.
- Don't give a pass to an adviser from an affinity group. Just because others you know trust him doesn't mean you should.
- Be careful of an adviser who's photographed with Nancy Pelosi, past presidents, or Bono. That much hobnobbing, though not always a rat sign, is a distraction from real work. Hobnobbing is a huge time, energy, and money drain.
- Be skeptical of fanciful life stories. These are easily faked. If something about their history contradicts, don't hire the adviser. Someone who'll tell a white lie about their past will tell a bigger lie with your money.

You want to hire an adviser based on their financial decision making, and that alone. Other considerations don't matter. And if something that doesn't matter is part of the sales pitch, be super suspicious.

## Don't Let Anyone in Between You and the Decision Maker

Only you can protect you. The SEC can't and likely never will—because they won't hire pirates. Your friends and family might be fooled too.

And even professionals won't always prefer an adviser with a rat-free set-up. To ensure you don't let anyone in the middle:

- Have a preference for SEC-registered advisers. The registration filing process can deter many would-be rats.
- Check the Form ADV for ratty inconsistencies. This isn't fail-proof, but it is an additional tool helping you.
- That said, understand what the SEC does and does not do. They register and regulate advisers and enforce securities laws, but they typically don't stop fraud ahead of time. And SEC registration is not, in itself, a sign your adviser isn't a rat.
- Avoid funds of funds and "feeder" funds. Besides being inefficient and generally more costly, you can't be sure what advisers a feeder fund hires on your behalf, or how well diversified the feeder fund is.
- If you use an "intermediator" to find an adviser, don't pay them an ongoing fee once you've found the adviser. Also, be sure to double check the due diligence the intermediator did, just like an institutional investor would.
- Give advisers you find via referral the same rigorous check you'd give an adviser you found on your own. Don't assume anyone else, no matter how smart or sophisticated, has done the level of checking you'd do yourself.
- But remember, a small auditing firm isn't a negating factor because they may not be vetting performance. But don't accept a financial audit from a large or small firm as a sign an adviser isn't a rat.

This won't work as well if you're considering a smaller adviser, but ask a larger adviser if they manage money for institutions. Madoff and Stanford both, though massive in scale, managed almost no money for large state pension funds or major corporate pension plans—unusual for an adviser who claimed to manage multiple billions. If an adviser passes the sniff test for a number of large institutional investors and particularly big pension plans, there's a better—but not perfect—chance they'll pass your sniff test, too.

# Hiring the Right Adviser

Now you know how not to hire a rat. But that's just the first step to finding a good adviser. You want someone whose interests are fully aligned with yours and who you can feel confident will make good decisions on an ongoing basis. But how can you know that?

The following is a list of questions I advise all clients ask advisers—whether of their current adviser or of one they're considering hiring. The answers give you a clearer idea of how your adviser operates, how they make decisions, and whether they're the best choice for you. Call your adviser and ask, or type these up and bring them with you the next time you meet. You'll either feel more confident in your adviser, or you'll discover you should find someone else who does make you feel confident. Either way—it's a good outcome.

SINCE ASSET ALLOCATION IS THE SINGLE MOST IMPORTANT DECISION MADE ON MY ACCOUNT . . .

- Who's responsible for making or recommending changes to my asset class mix? You? Another individual at your firm? Does the ultimate responsibility lie with me?
- Are my portfolio's reallocations primarily driven by your market views or my needs?
- How frequently is my overall portfolio allocation reviewed? (e.g., Only when I request it?)
- How has your recommended asset class mix changed over the last 10 years?
- What, specifically, do you monitor to forecast the market's direction?
- How does your market forecast affect your asset allocation recommendation?

**GLOBAL MARKET LEADERSHIP HAS ALWAYS AND WILL CONTINUE TO SHIFT OVER TIME . . .**

- Who's responsible for making or recommending changes to my portfolio's domestic versus foreign mix?
- How do you (or your firm) determine when and how much to underweight or overweight the US equity market?
- How do you (or your firm) decide which countries to invest in, and which to avoid?
- Who specifically makes these decisions?

**OVERALLOCATING TO THE WRONG EQUITY STYLE CAN SERIOUSLY HAMPER PERFORMANCE . . .**

- What is your firm's equity style? Large or small cap, growth or value?
- Will the style mix be static, or will there be ongoing changes?
- What would make you/your firm recommend a shift in or out of small cap stocks? Large cap? Value? Growth?
- What would make you/your firm recommend a shift in or out of specific sectors?
- Who is responsible for making asset style decisions or recommendations? What's their history of making these decisions?

**THE RIGHT MANAGER'S INTERESTS ARE FULLY ALIGNED WITH MINE . . .**

- Are you a Registered Investment Adviser or are you a broker? Are you registered with the SEC?
- Aside from what I pay you directly, what other compensation do you receive? (For example, commissions from insurance products, incentives for selling stocks and bonds from your firm's inventory, spreads on the sale of bonds, etc.)
- How can you demonstrate your firm's wealth management capability? For example, can I see GIPS-verified performance history for your clients' accounts?

Ultimately, who you hire is your decision. You have to protect yourself. Market volatility can be tough to take, but every bear market is followed by a bull market. You can overcome bear markets with some time and toughness. But if you hire a rat who successfully embezzles, you may never see a dime of your hard-earned money again. Don't let it happen to you. Knowing the signs of financial fraud is your ultimate defense against hiring a rat.

# Further Reading

Why do investors fall for financial fraud? These excellent books can help you understand some of the psychology behind investing and investors. See if you can spot some of your own madness.

## DOOMED TO REPEAT?

- *Extraordinary Popular Delusions and the Madness of Crowds* by Charles MacKay (Wilder Publications 2009). This classic, first published in 1841, is a must-read for modern investing enthusiasts.
- *Markets, Mobs & Mayhem: How to Profit from the Madness of Crowds* by Robert Menschel (Wiley 2005).
- *Mania, Panics, and Crashes: A History of Financial Crises* by Charles P. Kindleberger (Wiley 2000).

These books won't help you avoid fraudsters, but they're great books every investor should read and have.

## REQUIRED READING

- *A Monetary History of the United States 1867–1960* by Milton Friedman and Anna Schwartz (Princeton University Press 1963).
- *Capitalism and Freedom* by Milton Friedman (University of Chicago Press 1962).
- *Reminiscences of a Stock Operator* by Edwin Lefevre (Wiley 1923).
- *The Way the World Works* by Jude Wanniski (Simon & Schuster 1983).

# Appendix A
## Asset Allocation — Risk & Reward

Understanding market history can help you avoid con artists by understanding what's reasonable to expect. Table A.1 shows historic returns for a variety of asset allocations, as well as the largest gains and losses for each.

# Table A.1 Asset Allocation - Risk & Reward
## S&P 500 Rolling 12 Month Total Returns, January 1926 through December 2008

| | Largest 12 Month Rolling Loss | Average 12 Month Rolling Loss* | Average Return Since 1926 | Average 12 Month Rolling Gain** | Largest 12 Month Rolling Gain | Percent of 12 Month Periods Negative | Percent of 12 Month Periods Positive |
|---|---|---|---|---|---|---|---|
| 100% Stocks | −67.9% | −13.9% | 12.2% | 21.6% | 160.6% | 26.5% | 73.5% |
| 80% Stocks 20% Bonds | −54.5% | −10.8% | 10.5% | 18.1% | 130.1% | 25.2% | 74.8% |
| 70% Stocks 30% Bonds | −47.9% | −9.2% | 10.2% | 16.5% | 114.8% | 24.5% | 75.5% |
| 60% Stocks 40% Bonds | −41.2% | −7.8% | 9.6% | 14.8% | 99.5% | 23.1% | 76.9% |
| 50% Stocks 50% Bonds | −34.5% | −6.1% | 8.9% | 13.3% | 84.3% | 22.6% | 77.4% |
| 40% Stocks 60% Bonds | −27.9% | −4.5% | 8.2% | 11.6% | 69.0% | 20.4% | 79.6% |
| 30% Stocks 70% Bonds | −21.2% | −4.2% | 7.6% | 10.0% | 53.7% | 16.9% | 83.1% |
| 20% Stocks 80% Bonds | −14.5% | −3.2% | 6.9% | 8.8% | 46.0% | 15.5% | 84.5% |
| 100% Bonds | −13.2% | −2.3% | 5.6% | 7.4% | 48.8% | 17.5% | 82.5% |

Legend: ■ Largest Rolling 12 Month Loss ■ Average (Mean) Since 1926 ■ Largest Rolling 12 Month Gain

- 100% Stocks: 160.6%, 12.2%, −67.9%
- 80% Stocks 20% Bonds: 130.1%, 10.9%, −54.5%
- 70% Stocks 30% Bonds: 114.8%, 10.2%, −47.9%
- 60% Stocks 40% Bonds: 99.5%, 9.6%, −41.2%
- 50% Stocks 50% Bonds: 84.3%, 8.9%, −34.5%
- 40% Stocks 60% Bonds: 69.0%, 8.2%, −27.9%
- 30% Stocks 70% Bonds: 53.7%, 7.6%, −21.2%
- 20% Stocks 80% Bonds: 46.0%, 6.9%, −14.5%
- 100% Bonds: 48.8%, 5.6%, −13.2%

Source: S&P 500 Stock Index/US 10 Year Government Bond Index; Global Financial Data. The S&P 500 Index is a capitalization-weighted, unmanaged index that measures 500 widely held US common stocks of leading companies in leading industries, representative of the broad US equity market. The performance of selected stocks is presented inclusive of dividends.

* For 12 month periods with a loss
** For 12 month periods with a gain

# Appendix B
## Same But Different—Accounting Fraud

If you're an investor—any size—you must watch for financial fraud. But if you're a business owner, particularly a small business owner, you're in danger of accounting fraud. These are the simple cases you read about endlessly where the trusted bookkeeper has, over perhaps 20 years, quietly bilked a small fortune. Maybe more than $100,000, but usually not much more than $1 million. (Though one relatively talented con, Lynda Fratis, got away with almost $2 million during her five years as bookkeeper for Boogie's Aspen—a posh clothing boutique in Aspen. She's since been convicted.)[1]

Small business owners may believe they're immune. After all, their little business may not make enough to be embezzled. Also, they're more likely to have a small staff and a bookkeeper they either know or come to know very well and trust implicitly. It's larger firms who must worry—where faceless staff is more likely to bilk, right?

Exactly backward. You rarely hear about this kind of accounting fraud hitting large, publicly traded firms. And, in many ways, it's similar to financial Ponzi fraud—it's all about who has access. Overwhelmingly, the bookkeeper who bilks is responsible for both incoming and out-going checks as well as overall accounting (which is a set-up you see in smaller firms, not larger firms). The way to keep this from happening is to separate the function—just as you'd separate decision maker from custody. You have an accounts payable person, a separate accounts receivable person, and a third doing overall accounting.

Then, the only way they can embezzle is if they collude—though it's less likely. Two people can easily collude, but a third means more opportunities for the con to blow up. Larger firms will simply, by definition, have more staff and defined departments, which makes this con much more difficult.

## Bitter Bilkers

Another interesting feature about these types of fraud: Unlike financial fraud, accounting embezzlers are most often women. Google "book-keeper bilked," and 9 of 10 stories are about female accountants. Why? Same reason why money managers are typically male—just a function of societal evolution, nothing more. The accountant embezzlers have the function of being highly trusted by the CEO—they and the staff are always shocked to find out the nice bookkeeper has been bilking them for a decade.

Frequently, you see the embezzlers are simply bitter. Maybe they feel underpaid relative to others at the firm. Maybe they're angry the top-dog sales guys are making big bucks and they're not—and passive aggressively start taking a bit to make up for what they view as an injustice. Maybe they don't see themselves as *stealing*—they see themselves as taking what they should have rightfully gotten otherwise. Meanwhile, they're seen as nice, trustworthy people who don't kick up a fuss—that's their façade.

## Tiny Sips, Long Scams

This fraud isn't hard to accomplish. If you're responsible for incoming and outgoing checks, you maybe set up some fake vendors, which are really all you. You write some checks to the fake vendor, directing them to accounts you control. If you're smart, you change up the fake vendors occasionally. If asked about Vendor X by the CEO, they've gone out of business and you can't find them anymore. You've since moved on to Vendor Y. You don't take huge amounts all at once; you sip a little at a time—which is why these scams can last as long as they do.

In a firm that doesn't grow much (partially because the bookkeeper is embezzling), it's hard to out the embezzler. But, if a firm grows, eventually the CEO may want to add staff and separate the accounting functions into smaller and specific functions so the embezzler can't keep up the game. Or they hire an outside auditor who discovers the embezzlement. That's when the con can blow up.

The way to prevent this brand of scam is easy—separate responsibility for incoming and outgoing money. Even for a small firm, it shouldn't be hard. Instead of one full-time accountant, hire two part-timers who have other responsibilities. Better yet, have yet a third, wholly non-connected party audit the whole business. But if you separate incoming from outgoing, and the responsible parties can't collude, you've protected yourself pretty well.

# Appendix C
## Minds That Made the Market

Looking for more context on some of the characters—famous and infamous—mentioned in this book? This Appendix includes excerpted content from my 1993 book *100 Minds That Made the Market*, reprinted with permission from John Wiley & Sons.

Excerpted biographies include:

1. Ivar Kreuger (mentioned in Chapters 1 and 5).
2. Richard Whitney (mentioned in Chapter 1 and 4).
3. Walter F. Tellier (mentioned in Chapter 3).
4. Hetty Green (mentioned in Chapter 5).
5. James M. Landis (mentioned in Chapter 5).
6. Joseph P. Kennedy (mentioned in Chapter 5).

# Ivar Kreuger: He Played with Matches and Got Burned

Matches. They're cheap, readily available, necessary—and the basis for one of the most intricate and profitable financial schemes of the twentieth century. Swedish Match King Ivar Kreuger masterminded a world-wide scheme in which he essentially borrowed money from Americans to loan millions to European countries in exchange for their match franchises. At his pinnacle in the late 1920s, he controlled 75 percent of the world's match manufacturing—a virtual world monopoly! Ultimately, a lack of liquidity, too many secrets, and careless mistakes led to his demise, so in 1932 he shot himself in the chest to avoid public scrutiny. Once hailed as a financial genius, historians still wonder whether he was a pioneer, crazy, or just a crook.

Key to Kreuger's plan was his appearance, his façade. From the beginning his goal was to gain the confidence of American lending sources on Wall Street. With gray-green eyes, pallid, porous skin, and a pursed mouth, he met Wall Street's every expectation of a respectable businessman. He knew that if he looked and acted right, he would be granted credit. Kreuger appeared impeccably dressed in expensive yet uniform suits, accompanied by a cane and dark hat to cover his balding head. He was quiet but well-spoken, cultured, well-mannered, and mildly forceful. He courted Wall Street, eventually winning over top investment bankers who forked over hundreds of millions to his supposedly solid firm— at a time when a hundred million mattered. But they didn't know he was a phony, full of contradictions.

After his death, Wall Street's vision of the reserved, respectable Match King was shattered. To start with, Kreuger was plagued by multiple blackmailings for reasons unknown. Probably at least some of them

Source: "Europe's Newest Wizard of Finance," *Review of Reviews*, Vol. 79: April 1929, pp. 24–25; Manfred George, *The Case of Ivar Kreuger: An Adventure in Finance*, Jonathan Cape, LTD., 1933, pp. 256; John Lloyd Parker, *Unmasking Wall Street*, The Stratford Co., Publishers, 1932, pp. 154–187; Robert Shaplen, *Kreuger: Genius and Swindler*, Alfred A. Knopf, 1960; "The Collapse of the Kreuger Legend," *Literary Digest*, Vol. 113: May 7, 1932, pp. 36–39; "Why the House of Kreuger Fell," *Literary Digest*, Vol. 115: February 4, 1933, p. 40.

were his many mistresses—he had one in almost every major European city and kept over a dozen regular allowances! And that wasn't all. Kreuger, who had his first love affair at 15 with a woman twice his age (his mother's friend), kept a little black book filled with women's names—each had her own page detailing her personality, likes and dislikes, how much she cost—and whether she was worth it!

He kept drawers full of expensive brooches, cigarette cases, gold purses, watches, silks, and perfumes for his one-night stands. If he tired of one, he tossed her an envelope filled with stocks! Kreuger remained a bachelor, he said, because marriage and the honeymoon required "at least eight days, and I haven't got time."

His business practices, a later audit revealed, were equally shocking. He alone supplied the figures for his books, juggling numbers in his head even when his Stockholm-based holding company, Kreuger and Toll, went international. Kreuger conducted business through his own accounts to eliminate or create assets and liabilities and shift them from one firm to another.

Like his books, Kreuger made acquiring match factories and franchises an art form. Typically, to seize a factory, he would sell his own better-quality matches in the targeted factory's locale at current prices, thereby taking the market away from the local source without price-cutting. Then, once he had hurt the local source, he sent phony "independent" buyers to make ridiculously low offers on the factory, which would discourage the owners. Afterwards, when the offers had been rejected, he came in with his own better offers, which now seemed good to the owners. Once the factory was seized cheaply, he would again drop the quality of matches in the local market.

Franchises were secured by loaning countries like France and Germany millions at good rates and great terms; thereby securing long-term match franchises. An occasional bribe or two to the right official sometimes pushed agreements along. One of his greatest coups was loaning France $75 million at 5 percent after World War I, when American financiers like the House of Morgan were tightening their purse strings. He also bought hefty amounts of French bonds to stabilize the falling franc—and secure for himself a French match monopoly!

After bribing necessary politicians, the deal was approved in 1927, and he got a 20-year franchise—which would last longer than he would.

To keep confidence in his firm secure, Kreuger made sure his securities always paid high dividends. Sometimes, he quietly bought shares in one of his match companies, then sold them for profit to another company within his trust, inflating their value, claiming a profit en route, and enabling him to declare higher dividends. For fear of losing Wall Street's confidence, high dividends were paid right until the very end, even when Kreuger could barely afford them. Each time he issued stock in his firms, the stock's worth was always based on exaggerated business volume. That is to say, he commonly cooked the books. He was said to have inflated earnings to the tune of $250 million between 1917 and 1932!

Born in 1880 and trained as an engineer, Kreuger worked as a bridge builder, a real estate agent, and a steel salesman before realizing, "I cannot believe that I am intended to spend my life making money for second-rate people." In 1908, he formed Kreuger and Toll, an architectural-real estate firm, and five years later its subsidiary, United Match Factories, taking over two match manufacturing factories his father and uncle owned. Within four years, Kreuger, who ate little, believing it made him lazy, swallowed Sweden's largest match firms. He built a vertical trust whose securities were considered golden.

Throughout his career, Kreuger remained outwardly charming, but toward the end, his inner, eerie coldness began to seep from beneath his façade. He grew nervous. His smile weakened to the point of numbness. His handshake grew clammy. He spent money impulsively, collecting things like leather suitcases, canes, and cameras rather than art, as was customary among millionaires. And he spent money—lots of it—in desperate speculative deals that might right his desperate situation. That speculative trait is common among crooks in deep trouble.

The 1929 Crash was the beginning of the end for Kreuger. While his securities survived the crash relatively well, he had lent and borrowed too much—and the Crash caused a tight money flow. Instead of cutting back dividends or pulling in loans to conserve cash, which he felt would have sparked fatal rumors, he forged ahead on what auditors called "an orgy of financial ventures"—the most famous of which was his counterfeiting scheme. He had 42 Italian government bonds and five promissory notes printed, representing $142 million. As soon as he received them, he locked himself in his private top-floor Stockholm Match Palace and forged the names of Italian officials, spelling one official's name three different ways to make the securities look "authentic." Later, his accountants entered the phony bonds in the books.

By March, 1932, Kreuger had fallen apart at the seams. He had a nervous breakdown, couldn't sleep, answered imaginary telephone calls and door knocks, fumbled for answers regarding non-existent cash balances, and, finally, transferred money and securities into relatives' names. He wrote a couple of notes, one of which said, "I have made such a mess of everything that I believe this is the best solution for all concerned."

Then, in his business-like fashion, Kreuger lay down on his bed fully dressed, unbuttoned his pin-striped jacket and vest, and with his left hand held a handgun, purchased the day before, to his silk monogrammed shirt. He pulled the trigger and died almost instantaneously.

The Match King swindled some $250 million from American investors before his kingdom toppled. Yet he managed to build and operate a highly leveraged empire that lasted some 15 years. In many ways the 1929 Crash was only incidental to his story. As a basic crook and swindler he probably would have ended up in the same place before long anyway. You can't keep a debt-driven phony house of cards standing forever. No one ever has. He is just one more of the many wild and extravagant, womanizing Wall Streeters who was doomed to failure by his greater love of fast money and the things it would buy than of the actual processes of investing, owning, and running businesses.

# Richard Whitney: Wall Street's Juiciest Scandal

It was October 24, 1929—Black Thursday—when the tall and arrogant Richard Whitney, Wall Street's best-known broker, strode across the New York Stock Exchange floor to the US Steel specialist's post and uttered the most famous phrase in Stock Exchange history, "I bid 205 for 10,000 Steel." Stock prices were imploding and Steel could be bought for under 200, but by bidding what the stock was last sold for, Whitney breathed much-needed confidence onto the floor that day. People figured if Steel wasn't sliding, maybe others wouldn't.

Equipped with millions from a Morgan consortium, Whitney continued buying other blue-chip stocks, always in huge amounts at the price of the previous sales. Within minutes, he racked up some $20 million in orders, and then the market rallied—for a while. "Richard Whitney Halts Panic," read the headlines.

Overnight, fame found Whitney, the acting president of the NYSE. The press reported his every move, the New York Stock Exchange post where he uttered his first famous bid was retired from the floor and ceremoniously presented to him, and then Whitney was elected president of the Stock Exchange. He literally became Wall Street's voice and respected statesman. Whitney had a magnificent reputation to uphold.

While he came out of the Crash with "increased faith in this marvelous country of ours," he also came out of it poor. Years later he said he lost $2 million in the Crash. But he never had any large personal fortune to fall back on. His firm, Richard Whitney & Co., had high overhead and serviced a small, elite clientele, mainly JP Morgan & Co. It grossed more prestige than money—annual profits amounted to only $60,000.

By 1931, his firm's net worth was about $36,000, excluding over a million he had personally borrowed from his brother George, a Morgan partner. It continued downhill from there—he borrowed from JP

Source: John Brooks, *Once in Golconda*. Harper Colophon Books, 1970, pp. 230–287; Matthew Josephson, *The Money Lords*. Weybright and Talley, Inc., 1972, pp. 90–107, 125–128, 173–184; Humphrey B. Neill, *The Inside Story of the Stock Exchange*. B.C. Forbes & Sons Publishing Company, Inc., 1950, pp. 239, 252, 254, 260–263; "Richard Whitney, 86, Dies; Headed Stock Exchange." *New York Times*. Dec. 6, 1974, p. 42:1.

Morgan & Co., again and again from his brother, and then he fell further, borrowing from lesser brokers, from floor specialists, and from anyone on the exchange floor who would lend money against his prior great reputation. But folks in general didn't realize the extent of his borrowing.

Whitney remained optimistic, taking faith in applejack (a backwoods-style booze) of all things! No, he didn't hit the bottle—instead he prepared for Prohibition's repeal by taking over a chain of New Jersey distilleries. In 1933, he and a brokerage partner organized Distilled Liquors Corporation to make "New Jersey Lightning," which they thought could become America's next craze. While he waited for the craze to catch on, Whitney talked his creditors into extending his loans and borrowed still more from people he barely knew. Banks, at this point, were of no use, for he had no collateral.

When the repeal became effective, Distilled Liquors, which he bought between 10 and 15, jumped to 45. Had Whitney sold out he could have paid off everyone but his brother and worried about George later. But he had gambler's fever and bad judgment, and, thus, held on. Predictably, Whitney's luck soured as Distilled Liquors lagged for a lack of buyers. The more it sagged, the more Whitney scrounged to support the stock price—just barely above $10.

He was desperate now—if the stock declined, his outstanding bank loans would be called in for deficient collateral—and a desperate man does desperate things. In 1936, having run out of suckers to borrow from, and as word of his finances spread, Whitney became a swindler. Still treasurer of the New York Yacht Club, he took over $150,000 in Yacht Club bonds to fraudulently use as collateral against a $200,000 bank loan. He had gotten away with a similar scheme in 1926 when he "borrowed" bonds from his father-in-law's estate and replaced them three years later, with no one the wiser.

All rationality gone, Whitney embezzled the New York Stock Gratuity Fund (a multi-million dollar mutual-benefit arrangement for the families of deceased members). It was easy. He was one of its six trustees and its broker. So when the fund decided to sell $350,000 in bonds and buy a like amount of another bond issue, Whitney sold the bonds, placed the orders on the new ones, bought them, but then, instead of delivering them to the Gratuity Fund, he took the bonds to a bank as collateral for a personal loan! He repeated this scam over and over again, and within nine months, the fund was missing over $1 million in cash and bonds!

By 1937, the missing securities were discovered by the Gratuity Fund trustees. They asked for their property, and, after a few days and a cockamamie story about paperwork delaying delivery, Whitney returned the loot by the seat of his pants. The seat of his pants, meanwhile, was actually his brother George, who himself had to borrow the money from fellow Morgan partner Thomas Lamont.

Finally, the Exchange got wise to Whitney, dug into his books, and discovered his shady deals. But even then, he had hope. He reasoned with the Exchange and promised to sell his NYSE seat in return for dropped charges. "After all, I'm Richard Whitney. I mean the Stock Exchange to millions of people." In the end, completely oblivious to what was right and wrong, Whitney withdrew over $800,000 in customers' securities from his firm's account and, within four months, gathered some $27 million via 111 loans. He literally approached strangers on the Exchange floor, even prior enemies, holding out his hand and asking for money!

Whitney got 5 to 10 years at Sing-Sing and an injunction banned him from the securities industry forever. During sentencing, he looked haggard, his hands twitched, and he blushed when he was called a "public betrayer."

The aftermath of Whitney was even more pathetic. During his prison sentence, Distilled Liquors went bankrupt and his prestigious US Steel specialist's post, where he made his famous bid, was auctioned off for five bucks. Fellow inmates called him Mr. Whitney and sought his autograph— Whitney always obliged. A model prisoner, he was paroled in 1941, then stayed with relatives. For a while, he managed a family dairy farm in Barnstable, Massachusetts, then dropped out of sight permanently, and died at 86 in 1974 at his daughter's home. His brother repaid all his debts.

As Stock Exchange president, Whitney not surprisingly fought against government-guided stock market reform, calling the Exchange a "perfect institution." He said members had the "courage to do those things which are right, regardless of how unpopular they may be for the time being," and, thus, were capable of policing themselves. This was obviously quite untrue and, ironically, we have Whitney to attest to the fact.

# Walter F. Tellier: The King of the Penny Stock Swindles

Unsophisticated investors didn't stand a chance against Walter Tellier and his band of boiler room bandits. High-pressure sales tactics and grade-A sucker lists fueled Tellier's well-oiled machine, which churned out millions of worthless, irresistibly cheap "penny stocks" in exciting, "sure-fire" opportunities like uranium mines and Alaskan telephone circuits. When Tellier was finally caught and the gig was up, investors were left about a million in the hole and rocked by yet another Wall Street scandal.

Originally a cosmetics salesman from Hartford, Connecticut, and born about 1900, Tellier peddled securities in the middle of the great 1920s bull market. When the 1929 Crash hit, he relied on the buy-now, pay-later plan to attract salaried workers with meager savings and big dreams. By 1931, his outstanding salesmanship paid off—Tellier was able to start his own firm with a couple of thousand bucks distributing various issues for Wall Street brokerage houses. Two years later, one of the houses he worked for suggested he open a New York branch. He did, and business boomed, so he closed down the Hartford office and moved to the Big Apple to specialize in wholesaling securities to brokers. No sooner was he settled in his new office than he was indicted on conspiracy charges and mail fraud—but this case was later dismissed.

Soft-spoken yet aggressive, Tellier laid low, selling securities legally (presumably), making moderate money until the 1950s bull market—of which he took full advantage. He began pumping out penny stocks to freshman investors, a new market recently rediscovered by Wall Street and loved for its wide-eyed enthusiasm, gullibility, no-questions-asked loyalty, and hope for miracles. Guys like Charles Merrill, and much of Wall Street, loved these investors for the commission-based opportunity they represented—and served them well. But Tellier touted miracles

Source: Hillel Black, *The Watchdogs of Wall Street*. William Morrow and Company, 1962, pp.20–56,79,84–89; Burton Crane, " 'Penny' Uranium Stock Expert Blasts S.E.C. and 'Fraud' Talk." *New York Times*. Nov. 4, 1955, p. 43:4; "Tellier is Barred in New York State." *New York Times*. July 6, 1956, p. 31:5; "Broker is Jailed in $900,000 Fraud." *New York Times*. April 13, 1957.

by the dozen—miracles for only fifteen cents to a half-dollar per share! Tellier served these guys too, like a baked pig with an apple in its mouth.

The validity of his "miracles" is one story—one that you can read about in any of the sources listed below—but his method of dumping them on the public is a much better story. Tellier didn't invent boiler rooms, but he made fine use of them, as described in the book, *The Watchdogs of Wall Street*. Boiler rooms were no different from any con game, except they were out to swindle in the name of Wall Street! Typically found in dingy lofts, several flights of stairs from any outsider's view, the rooms themselves were furnished in a makeshift fashion with boxes for benches, propped-up plywood as conference tables, cramped cubicles with telephones for the con men, harsh bare bulbs, and cardboarded windows. The victims on the other end of the phone line assumed they were talking to one of America's top financial leaders from one of those plush Wall Street offices.

The men who made the boiler rooms boil were often hardened criminals who'd served time for serious crimes; entry-level positions were filled by college kids looking to pay for tuition. Ties and shirts tossed aside in the sweltering heat, the "coxeys," or entry-level swindlers, made first contact with customers, calling from lists of potential suckers. Some had already received Tellier's direct mailings so they were familiar with Tellier's name when they received the call. To make the initial good impression, the coxey would say he was calling "from Wall Street," then proceed to make wild claims about the penny stocks. "Mr. So and So, just make a small purchase and you'll see what we can do for you." This call might bring in between $50 and $100.

The lists would then be forked over to the "loaders," the more experienced cons. It was their job to find out how much their target was really worth—that is, if he mortgaged his house and borrowed from every friend and family member. If the person held blue-chip stocks, the loader talked him into selling them for a Tellier issue. Finally, "superloaders" or "dynamiters," the highest paid and most persuasive in the scam, could convince their target to steal if necessary to buy a hot stock! They'd slyly confide "hot" tips they "just learned from the floor" or "picked up in the board room."

Amidst the cigar smoke and cigarette butts, boiler rooms in 1956 alone parted tens of thousands of suckers from some $150 million. And the cons were well taken care of for their efforts: A sales manager might take $150,000 from managing one boiler room, and one loader once made $75,000 in six months. While the boiler rooms pumped out the goods, Tellier was busy twisting securities laws to protect himself and not his victims, as in the case of the full-disclosure provision of the Truth in Securities Act of 1933. In this case, the law allowed an issue to be exempt from full registration if it sold for under $300,000, which ironically was ideal for penny stock scams. So, of course, his issues typically totaled $295,000.

He also plunged into advertising, promoting his issues on radio stations and in major dailies, like the *New York Times*. His print ads featured a coupon to clip and send in for more information—a seemingly innocent promotion that in reality supplied his boiler room staff with names and addresses. Later, it was said Tellier sold his infamous sucker-lists to an investment advisory firm after the government nabbed him.

But until he was nabbed, Tellier walked with his head held high and projected the utmost respectability. At North American Securities Administrators conventions—filled with the very officials who were supposed to police Tellier-type activities—he threw lavish cocktail parties that became the highlight of the conventions. He became a respectable family man living in lush Englewood, New Jersey—home of Morgan partners for years. He joined Westchester Country Club (where he sold some stocks to clubhouse employees), lavishly furnished his office, and drove a Cadillac. Slightly balding, Tellier was very conscious of appearances and dressed to impress.

By 1956, he was impressing a federal grand jury with his utter disregard for SEC regulation. Despite his claim that he was "the most investigated person in the world" because of his prominence in the penny stock industry, the next year Tellier & Company was closed down, and Tellier was barred from trading in stocks in New York and New Jersey, where most of his victims lived. He was charged with fraudulent stock promotion practices in the sale of uranium and Alaskan telephone securities that swindled investors out of about $1 million. During his trial, he tried to bribe a government witness with $250,000 but was unsuc-cessful. In 1958, he received a four-and-a-half-year prison term and an $18,000 fine. After that, the king of penny stocks was never heard from again.

In most penny stock scams there is a consistent phenomenon: The brokerage firm carrying the issue is the only place where you can buy or sell the stock. This lets the firm control the market. For example, in a usual securities deal, there is a syndicate put together by the lead under-writer, and the syndicate members each carry a piece of the overall deal. Then, various syndicate members agree to "make a market" in the stock after the deal is complete by competing against each other to buy and sell the stock. In this and every other market, it is competition that ensures honesty. In a regular market you can buy a stock from dealer X and sell it through dealer Y. And, if you don't like X or Y, there are also dealers U, W, and Z. But in a penny stock scam there is no other market. There is no syndicate on the original deal, and there is no after-market of competitive brokerage firms—only the guy who stuck you with the stock in the first place. So when he sells it to you at $1.50 one month, you may find you can only sell it back—to him— for a quarter the next month. There is no place else to go; no competition for your stock.

Another trick of the penny stock guys is to break up the country, or even a state, into geographies. In some of the areas, they start selling the issue. A few months later, they start buying it back at a fraction of the price, while, at the same time, selling it in another geography to a new set of suckers at a much higher price, often even higher than the orig-inal offering price. They tell this new second set of suckers that the stock has been going up since it was issued—because it is so hot. Tellier pioneered all of these methods via the boiler room.

Tellier led the penny stock scam phenomenon, and it has replayed almost nonstop ever since, and largely in the same form as when Tellier did it. The main difference recently has been that the boiler rooms look just like standard brokerage offices and the crooks have learned how to dress. Dressing like a businessman and being able to scam face-to-face increases the image of respectability and lets you get away with bigger swindles. Tellier should have been smart enough to see this, but he was a pioneer, and every industry gets better with practice.

Whether it is Robert Brennan advertising his New Jersey-based First Jersey Securities scams on national television, any of a host of penny ante Colorado-based scam masters, or the new "king," Meyer Blinder, and his devoted army of arm twisters (also in Colorado, and now, having been driven out of America, pulling the same scams overseas), the penny stock arena has evolved into one of the prime places where out-and-out crooks work their magic in the modern securities world. Tellier would be proud.

# Hetty Green: The Witch's Brew, Or . . . It's Not Easy Being Green

How would you picture Wall Street's first female finagler? It can't possibly compare with the miserly, eccentric Hetty Green who shrewdly turned a $6 million inheritance into $100 million. Not quite the business-schooled, gray-suit type, Green shrouded herself in foul-smelling black, outdated dresses in which she sewed untold securities. Donned daily in the same attire—complete with grimy black cotton gloves, bonnet, shabby umbrella, and cape—Hetty scurried between raunchy flats and her headquarters, the Chemical National Bank vault, fleeing the money-hungry spirits who "pursued" her. Eating graham crackers, oatmeal, and, on occasion, unwrapped ham sandwiches from the filthy folds of her packets, Hetty sat cross-legged on the vault floor clipping coupons—stuffing them down her bosom. Within months of her Wall Street arrival, the middle-aged eccentric became known as "the Witch of Wall Street."

Yet even a witch must possess an investment strategy—and hers was simple. In a pre-income tax world, she strove to make and keep 6 percent every year. To wit, Green operated under two rules. First, she never aimed for "big hits," preferring a great many good solid invest-ments with relatively safe returns. Second, Green was stingy.

"There is no secret in fortune making. I believe in getting in at the bottom and out at the top. All you have to do is buy cheap and sell dear, act with thrift and shrewdness, and be persistent. When I see a good thing going cheap because nobody wants it, I buy a lot of it and tuck it away."

Inherent in Green's thinking was that most folks consume their invest-ment harvests, but if you spend nothing, you keep it all, and it keeps com-pounding. If you compound $6 million at 6 percent for 51 years, without

Source: Peter Z. Grossman, "The Great Investors of the 20th Century," *Financial World*, June 15, 1982; Stewart H. Holbrook, *Age of the Moguls*. Doubleday & Co., Inc., 1953, pp. 340–342; John N. Ingham, *Biographical Dictionary of American Business Leaders*, 4 vols. Greenwood Press, 1983; Brian McGinty, "Hetty Green: The Witch of Wall Street," *American History Illustrated*, September 1988, pp. 30–31; Boyden Sparkes and Samule Taylor Moore, *Hetty Green: A Woman Who Loved Money*, Doubleday, Doran & Co., Inc., 1930.

spending any of your 6 percent, you get $117 million. And that's exactly what Green did. She became the richest women in America, but to accomplish her goal, as you will see, Green was also perhaps the most miserly.

Green bought stock heavily, but only in the depths of financial panics—and then, primarily railroad stocks. Otherwise, she bought real estate mortgages, government and municipal bonds, and other safe, income-oriented investments. Since she spent virtually nothing, she kept reinvesting at 6 percent. Stocks were the icing on her cake. She stepped into the breach of financial panics—her "harvest"— as she reveled at buying stocks from men gone broke. Never a late-bull market buyer, she simply bought in crashes, when no one else would. Considering her confidence and riveting results, one wonders whether she turned to women's intuition or, perhaps, insider information. A well-known example of her timely luck was her pullout from Knickerbocker Trust shortly before it failed in the 1907 Panic. Her clue? "The men in that bank are too good looking!" She bailed out, leaving her with abundant cash to loan sorry speculators.

Hetty was in the minority as the market's only woman—and she knew it. "I am willing to leave politics to men, although I wish women had more rights in business and elsewhere than they now have. I could have succeeded much easier in my career had I been a man. I find men will take advantages of women in business that they would not attempt with men. I found this so in the courts, where I have been fighting men all my life."

She hit Manhattan after a ghastly childhood and unsatisfying marriage. Born Henrietta Howland Robinson in 1834, Hetty's father was a determined fortune hunter, who married her mother's old New England money. While momma had a fairy-tale life in mind for Hetty—princes and the like—Hetty was Daddy's Girl, and daddy, Edward "Black Hawk" Robinson, was money's slave. Growing up in the vulgar whaling city of New Bedford, Massachusetts, Hetty watched her father build a shipping empire by exploiting people, forfeiting luxuries, and scrimping on necessities. Following in her father's footsteps, Hetty, the richest girl in town, was clad in rags and learned "never to give anyone anything, not even kindness."

The young ragamuffin scampered the wharves, absorbing dad's foul language, financial savvy, fierce temper, and frugal ways as her daintiness disintegrated. In 1865, with her mother, father, and aunt dead, Hetty inherited nearly $6 million—and a deranged demeanor. Black Hawk's mission succeeded: Hetty was left as determined and callous as he, primed for Wall Street, with a chartreuse dollar sign for a heart.

Hetty was adept at getting her way. When nagging failed, she went for the tears! When tears failed, she initiated lawsuits. The only thing wrong with lawsuits was the lawyer's fee: She hated lawyers' fees more than the men themselves. Regardless, she employed a steady stream of them, refusing to pay each and every one! "I had rather that my daughter should be burned at the stake than to have her suffer what I have gone through with lawyers." Once, she even paid a $50 registration fee to carry a revolver "mostly to protect myself against lawyers."

Hetty picked up market tips from her free-spending millionaire husband, Ned Green, who made money in the Philippine tea and silk trade. It's a wonder she married at all, as she eyed each suitor with suspicion. But, at the start, Ned had the upper hand—dangling Street savvy above Hetty's head. They were wed in 1867. Some say she married not for love, but for free financial advice—and room and board! Regardless, they had two kids—a boy and a girl—while Hetty made money in American gold bonds, largely due to Green's speculative skill. When the Panic of 1873 hit, Hetty was caught on the long side, watching her stocks depreciate. En route she learned her lesson well, vowing to always "harvest" panics from then on, and she did.

Ned Green was soon appalled by his wife's penny-pinching ways, such as replacing their fine china with decrepit, cracked dishes, and haggling local merchants on every penny. But Hetty was as fed up with her husband as he was with her. When his speculative luck failed, Hetty bailed him out at least three times—after the fourth, she washed her hands of him. While they remained married, they never shared their lives again in any form.

Hetty's only real love was money. By 1900, she was reputedly worth $100 million, earning $20,000 per day. With money piling up faster than she could put it to work, she feverishly bought railroads, such as the Ohio and Mississippi in 1887, but not before being completely informed of her investment and rethinking it overnight. And, if it didn't yield 6 percent, forget about it! In 1892, she formed the Texas Midland railroad, combining the smaller lines Waco & Northwestern—for which she had her son outbid a bitter enemy. For Hetty, the railroads were not only an income source, but a source of employment for her son, Ned.

Hetty groomed Ned as her successor, even paying his college tuition—only after securing his promise to stay single for 20 years after graduation. Ned was a momma's boy to the bone—as a kid, he resold his mother's newspaper each morning after she finished. Ned started as a clerk for her Connecticut River railroad, then graduated to overseeing her $5 million of Chicago real estate. As he raked in $40,000 per month for his mom, she paid him $3 per day—"training." Hetty, a proud mother, had aspirations for him—why, he could be another Jay Gould! But even with Ned, her love of money came first. When 14 years old, Ned injured his knee sledding downhill. Hetty fetched her shabbiest dress and waited unsuccessfully in line at a free medical clinic, after applying her useless treatment of hot sand and tobacco leaf poultices. When Ned's father learned of his son's unimproved condition, he sought a doctor without Hetty's consent, and paid $5,000 to have Ned's leg amputated—gangrene had set in.

Strive to get something for nothing—that was Hetty's motto. Following a stroke brought on by a fierce argument with a friend's cook, Green died in 1916 leaving behind a fortune—entirely in liquid assets—that she had acquired and protected ferociously. Attempting to keep her fortune within the confines of her immediate family—knowing that she couldn't take it with her—Green had constructed a restrictive will and prenuptial agreements to prevent in-laws from inheriting. Since her son and daughter had no children, her millions were eventually passed to more than 100 beneficiaries who never even knew Green.

Hetty teaches a lot of investment lessons. While her miserliness stands out as negative, her compounding success teaches us that frugality, when combined with reinvestment, is a powerful mechanism if even moderate rates of return can be achieved. Likewise, her insistence on safe 6 percent returns, while slightly low by modern standards, clearly points to the power of compound interest and the fact that most folks will do better getting a good safe return than gambling on a few risky and dramatic plays. If you happen to have $50,000 now in a tax-free retirement plan and could compound it at 15 percent per year for 50 years, as Hetty did her 6 percents, you would end up with more than $50 million. The power of compound interest—the witch's brew.

# James M. Landis: The Cop Who Ended Up in Jail

A hard-nosed, hard-driving, and hard-drinking law-professor-turned-securities-regulator forced a resistant Wall Street to prepare for drastic change following 1929. As a main architect of the Securities Act of 1933 and one of its first enforcers, James MacCauley Landis defined and directed that change and helped shape a new, regulated, and reformed Wall Street.

A chain smoker and workaholic who drove too fast and drank too much, Landis typified the staunch, serious, and overzealous policeman out to get his man. Standing 5'7", with thinning hair, tight lips, and big jowls—a real sourpuss face—he wore dowdy, rumpled suits and kept his hands stuffed in his pants pockets. Gulping black coffee and smoking two packs of Lucky Strikes each day, he was nicknamed "Cocksure" Landis for his self-assured arrogance and inability to take criticism.

Known as an independent thinker, Landis was called to Washington from his Harvard professorship and Cambridge home to help draw up the Securities Act in 1933. He wrote tough enforcement provisions, including making non-compliance of a subpoena a penal offense. He called for fines and prison terms for all parties involved with fraudulent securities sales, from company directors to underwriters to lawyers. Landis also devised a "stop order" that allowed the commission to freeze an issue if its paperwork looked suspicious. The legislation was a hit with the reform-hungry New Deal crowd and its popularity vaulted Landis into upper-crust capital circles. But back on Wall Street, the press said Landis symbolized "a New Deal brain-truster with somewhat radical tendencies and an inclination to go off half-cocked on high-sounding but impractical reforms."

Source: Maxine Block, ed., *Current Biography*. The H.W. Wilson Co., 1942, pp. 481–484; "James M. Landis Found Dead In Swimming Pool at His Home." *New York Times*, July 31, 1964, pp. 1:4; Mayer, Martin. *Wall Street: Men and Money*. Harper & Brothers Publishers, 1959, pp. 129, 236; "Nothing Much to Say." *Newsweek*, Vol. 62: Sept. 9, 1963, p. 31; Donald A. Ritchie, *James M. Landis: Dean of the Regulators*. Harvard University Press, 1980, pp. 43–91; Joel Seligman, *The Transformation of Wall-Street*. Houghton Mifflin Co., 1982, pp. 57–69, 79–89, 97–102; "The Careless Crusader," *Time*, Vol. 82: August 9, 1963, pp. 15–16.

Impractical or not, most of Wall Street adopted the new Securities Act, which went into full effect on July 7, 1933. That day, 41 firms filed statements with the Federal Trade Commission (FTC) Securities Division, the first agency to carry out the law. Together, the firms paid out $8,000 in registration fees to issue $80 million in stock after 20 days. It was the beginning of a new Wall Street—and Landis remained in Washington to make sure it stayed that way.

In 1933, just as he prepared to head back to Harvard, Landis was appointed to the FTC by President Franklin Roosevelt. He worked day and night—even keeping a cot in his office—to develop the rules and regulations that carried out the Securities Act. That year, he prevented or suspended 33 illegal issues. In 1934, when a senator's amendment created the Securities and Exchange Commission (SEC) to replace the FTC, Landis was named to that, too. He wrote most of the SEC's first opinions while serving under the first SEC chair, Joe Kennedy.

A year later, on the day before his 36th birthday in 1935, Landis took Kennedy's place as the $10,000-per-year SEC chairman. He promised to uphold Kennedy's cooperative stance with Wall Street as much as possible, while vowing to prosecute all stock frauds. For instance, he expelled stock operator Michael Meehan from three major stock exchanges on charges of manipulating stocks via "matched sales" in Bellanca Aircraft. The liberal press hailed him! Years later, he'd say, "The Securities and Exchange Commission has to be both a crack-down and a cooperating agency, depending on the circumstances. I don't think we have soft-peddled anything."

More than prosecuting individual violators, however, Landis was left the task of deconstructing what was then "the" corporate way of life—the holding company. The controversial and much-hated Public Utility Holding Act of 1935 called for giant holding companies to divest themselves of all subsidiaries not geographically or economi-cally linked. Trying to be Mr. Nice Guy and still uphold cooperation between government and business, Landis "suggested" the holding companies "voluntarily" divest themselves. But Wall Street hated him, and perhaps not without reason. All basic notions of capitalism are based on freedom, which at its most extreme means anyone can do anything, and pressure from Washington was restrictive and therefore threatening to Wall Street, which for 100 years had been the citadel of freedom in finance. The holding companies fought the law all the way from inception to passage, so they weren't about to voluntarily divest themselves of anything without a major legal battle.

Landis chose to convince them with a big splash—to make an example of the world's largest utility holding company, Electric Bond and Share Company. First he gave the company one more chance to register with the SEC by December 1, 1935. No luck; Electric Bond wouldn't budge. Then, two days after the deadline passed, the firm's president personally visited Landis to declare it would sue the SEC! That was when he struck: As the smug president strolled out of Landis' office, Landis picked up the phone and put down the meter to start a lawsuit he had prearranged before his visitor had arrived—before Electric Bond could get its suit started. Landis won. By January, 1937, the courts backed the SEC and demanded the holding companies comply with the legislation. Landis triumphantly declared the losers had "cut their own throats."

By 1937, Landis was tense and weary, with little family life to speak of. His wife regularly attended Washington social functions on her own. If someone asked for her husband, she'd reply, "What husband?" The marriage was crumbling, and he'd neglected his two daughters. His obsession with his work and booze was costing him his health—he suffered a series of bouts with influenza before the doctor demanded a lighter workload.

As much as he disliked the idea, Landis resigned in 1937 to return to Harvard Law School as dean. Unfortunately, he lingered in his SEC position—as a favor to Roosevelt, skipping a needed vacation—long enough to catch flak for that year's deep recession. Stock prices hit the lowest they'd been since the Great Depression, and the New York Stock Exchange president openly blamed the SEC. Landis retaliated, blaming the crisis on speculators who had returned to the market because of New Deal prosperity. What's better—prosperity with a few crooked speculators or depression with no opportunity but everyone on the up and up? Sort of makes you wonder if Landis didn't like it better with the world in depression.

Landis was remembered politically as a realist who didn't expect rapid change. By drafting and adhering to legislation, he expected reform to evolve gradually. He felt regulation was a process that would occur naturally—without harm to the economic process—if not made uniform and rigid.

For being such a careful and patient planner, Landis had an extremely erratic life. Besides his SEC career, at one point or another he: had his own law practice (Joe Kennedy was his number-one client); served as Civil Aeronautics Board chairman; reorganized and directed the Office of Civil Defense; authored a few books on law; served on the National Power Policy Commission; campaigned for President Roosevelt's third term; and, for a while, became active in local school politics. His love life was no less hectic. While married and working at Harvard, post-SEC, he fell in love with his married secretary. They eventually both divorced their first spouses and married each other.

Born in Tokyo in 1899, the son of Presbyterian missionaries, Landis came to America in 1912 to attend private school. By 1921 he worked his way through Princeton University as a justice of the peace and he received a law degree from Harvard in 1925. After clerking for the prestigious Supreme Court Associate Judge Louis Brandeis, he landed at Harvard as an assistant professor of law and made full professor at 26, the youngest in Harvard's history. From Harvard, he embarked on his Washington career.

Landis died in 1964 at age 64. He was found face down in his 40-foot-long swimming pool at his 10-room Westchester, New York, home—with traces of alcohol in his blood. Although he swam every day, it was rumored—falsely—that he'd committed suicide. Just days previously, Landis had been suspended from practicing law in New York State for a year because of a year-old conviction on income tax evasion. Imagine that! The head cop breaking the law. In 1963, Landis pleaded guilty to failing to file Federal income tax returns for the years between 1956 and 1960; he received 30 days in prison and paid some $92,000 in back taxes and fines. He didn't mean any harm, he'd said— he was just too busy. One doubts if the firms and people he pressed in his securities regulation career would have gotten very far with him had they used the same excuse.

Is the world a better place with all of the securities regulations that Landis helped put in place? Most folks assume so. But I don't think anyone can tell. The world is so fundamentally different now— almost 75 years after the first New Deal securities legislation—that it is impossible to say how the securities world would have evolved had the Roosevelt administration and Congress blinked five times, looked the other way, and avoided securities regulation until the securities markets naturally returned to higher prices. One could argue, as the New York Stock Exchange did, that prices might have returned to 1920s levels much faster without the presence of the SEC. But who knows? The world is what it is, and it is partly what it is because of the serious role Landis took in playing cop to Wall Street.

# Joseph P. Kennedy: Founding Chairman of the SEC

When you think of Joe Kennedy, you recall his legacy of political giants. What Wall Street notes, however, is a speculator who kicked and scratched his way to some $500 million—and the perks that went with it, like a well-respected name. But what the "Street" should remember is his role as the founding chairman of the Securities and Exchange Commission (SEC).

His story starts with his scrambling for millions—the kicking and scratching part. Kennedy was unrelenting and unscrupulous, a womanizer and social climber who was often in it for his ego. Whether it was taking a mayor's daughter for his wife or contributing to a president's campaign till in return for a political appointment or two, Kennedy had a fistful of strategic moves that took him wherever he wanted.

His drive was always a matter of pride. The carrot-topped son of a popular, small-time British-Irish politician wanted admittance to Boston's high society—which was, of course, impossible for a person of poor background. Perhaps that was why he wanted it so much—because it was so out of reach. This hunger produced a driven man who allowed nothing to get in the way of his ambitions. So, as a Harvard grad who almost played pro ball, Kennedy stormed into banking via his father's political connections. By age 25, in 1913, he was America's youngest bank president at a small bank his dad had formed.

Kennedy was charismatic. With his dynamic and amiable personality, freckle-faced Kennedy made a sprawling network of contacts that brought him a variety of jobs before he landed on Wall Street. First, he married well, winning the Boston mayor's daughter. The he ran a local pawnshop, dabbled in real estate, managed a Bethlehem Steel shipyard, served on a utility's board, and, finally, managed a brokerage office for Hayden, Stone and Company (long ago merged into Shearson).

Source: "Foreign Service: Chameleon & Career Man." National Affairs. *Time*, Vol. 30: Dec. 20, 1937, pp. 10–11; Alex Groner, *The History of American Business & Industry*. American Heritage Publishing Co., Inc., 1972, pp. 89–91, 97; John N. Ingham, *Biographical Dictionary of American Business Leaders*. 4 vols. Greenwood Press, 1983; Matthew Josephson, *The Money Lords*. Weybright and Talley, 1972, pp. 85–88, 176–185; David E. Koskoff, *Joseph P. Kennedy: A Life and Times*. Prentice-Hall, Inc., 1974; "Wall Street's New Boss 'Knows the Game.'" *Literary Digest*, Vol. 18: July 21, 1934, p. 36.

In 1923, Kennedy struck out on his own—"Joseph P. Kennedy, Banker"—and quickly established himself as a lone wolf on the Street, though he also worked with syndicates. Without conscience, but with a shrewd mind, Kennedy would "advertise the stock by trading it." When the public bought in, he pushed up its price and sold out; and then Kennedy sold short as the stock drifted back down to its normal price. He was a manipulator of unusual skill. Kennedy once told a friend, "It's easy to make money in this market. We'd better get in before they pass a law against it."

In a maneuver typical of Kennedy but unusual for most folks, Kennedy once returned a favor to a Yellow Cab executive when Yellow Cab stock was in the midst of a bear raid, having dropped from 85 to 50. Acting as the stock's sugar daddy, Kennedy set up shop in the Waldorf-Astoria running a shoring-up operation, which he warned his friend could cost as much as $5 million. The Waldorf was a convenient location for his unending string of floozies. There he installed a ticker tape, and, from his bedside, bought and sold Yellow Cab, using various brokers to conceal his position. He pushed the stock below 48, up to 62, down to 46, then stabilized it at 50 to confuse the bears. En route, instead of costing $5 million, it cost relatively little, and Kennedy claimed a hefty take for himself.

Always manipulating public relations to his much-loved family image, he said with false innocence, "I woke up one morning, exhausted, and I realized that I hadn't been out of that hotel room in seven weeks. My baby, Pat, had been born and was almost a month old, and I hadn't even seen her!" Such was the demeanor of the father of a future US president. Pat probably never noticed her father's absence, but poor Rose must have wondered where her hubby was and what he was doing. Presumably it wasn't merely the Yellow Cab stock operation that exhausted him in that bed. A few months later, when Yellow mysteriously plummeted again, it was Kennedy who was blamed by his former friend for the decline—and threatened with a punch in the nose! The presumption was that Kennedy, with his knowledge of the stock and its market, stepped back into the market and drove it down via short selling. No one ever knew for sure. But it's possible.

Befitting his personality—that of a social pariah—Kennedy took on Hollywood, where few Wall Streeters had ventured prior to the 1920s. During his cinematic stint, he financed a movie-theater chain. He later sold it to RCA for half a million and made two films, including a costly silent flop with actress-girlfriend Gloria Swanson. While Swanson actually ate the losses, Kennedy basked in free publicity, laughing off his million-dollar loss. What he really lost was a girlfriend, and there was always another one of those to be had.

In 1928, in a move of uncanny vision, Kennedy unloaded his movie securities for $5 million (to help create RKO) and did likewise for his other securities in preparation for hard times. With amazingly good timing, Kennedy said, "Only a fool holds out for the top dollar," and, when the Crash hit, he was able to watch the markets from a safe distance, keeping his fortune intact. In the 1929 Crash, while he held stocks that were hit, they were offset by an equal number of short positions that rose in value. The Crash left him unscathed. There is a legend, which he probably promoted at the time, that he sold short heavily as the market crashed and made a killing. Not true—merely legend. His short sales were a hedge, and he did not profit in a material way from the Crash. He maintained.

Meanwhile, he took stock of his life. Now that he had made his pile, he wanted to make it respectable. But he wasn't actually too successful at it. It would be up to his sons to truly salvage his reputation, which was far from sparkling. But he tried. He started out the only way he knew how—he made more connections. But this time, he went straight to the top, courting presidential hopeful Franklin Roosevelt by oiling his campaign fund with more than $150,000, which was a lot in those days. Of course, you never can have too much money, and, as the Kennedy and Roosevelt families grew closer, Kennedy borrowed Roosevelt's son to secure prestigious English Scotch franchises just before Prohibition was repealed. And he was somehow allowed to ship in the booze before the law was actually appealed for "medicinal" purposes! This is the period of Kennedy's life when he was tagged a "bootlegger," which was not terribly material to his wealth or life, but it was to his image.

When Roosevelt was elected, the mid–1930s became the self-proclaimed "President-maker's" favorite years. He was picked by Roosevelt and elected to chair the newly established Securities and Exchange Commission. Democrats shrieked at Kennedy's selection as an abomination. They figured he would do nothing to hamper the activities of his old friends on Wall Street. It was an appointment likened to letting the wolf out to guard the sheep. But Roosevelt was satisfied with Kennedy's promise to stay out of the market—and, the President mused, he "knows all the tricks of the trade!" Roosevelt supposedly muttered something to Kennedy's detractors to the effect that, "it takes a thief to catch a thief." Surprisingly, the charming Kennedy won over his harshest critics in his one year at the SEC, diligently outlawing most of the methods he had used to amass his fortune. Supposedly, Kennedy's knowledge of how to manipulate stocks was central to the New Deal version of how to reform the securities industry. Realistically, he may have been picked as a pay-off for his efforts and money on Roosevelt's behalf, and I haven't seen any evidence that his SEC functioning was more than perfunctory.

Still, Kennedy's SEC stint did much to scrub up his image. That allowed Roosevelt to move him on to a more prestigious position, US Ambassador to Great Britain—just what the doctor ordered for the Irishman who grew up with a chip on his shoulder!

As World War II ended, with the Roosevelt world gone and with Kennedy older and slower, he turned again to business, but this time he focused on real estate. His prime purchase was the world's largest commercial building, Chicago's Merchandise Mart—which he bought in 1945 for $13 million and that 2 years later was worth $75 million, throwing off more than $13 million cash, annually. Various estimates of his net worth in the mid-1960s place it on the high side of $200 to $400 million.

In some ways, the 1960s had to be the high point of his life as son, John, was elected president. But it was also the end, emotionally and physically. His heart started giving him problems and he suffered a stroke in 1961. Later, John's death was like a cloud over his heart. A series of heart attacks left him incapacitated for the first time in his life.

Robert's assassination in 1968 couldn't have helped. He died the next year, after funneling his fortune into intricate trust funds for his children and grandchildren to avoid Uncle Sam's take.

Kennedy was an enigma. A social climber, womanizer, mad scrambler, market manipulator, movie mogul, government regulator, Ambassador, real estate tycoon, and president's father. He is very hard to summarize briefly. But, whenever I think of Kennedy, I think of the many things he did in early eras that were taboo in later ones, and his ability to adhere to the social and legal mores of the day. You have to be reminded by the founding chairman of the SEC to honor the law. You have to also be reminded by Kennedy's evolving lifestyle and business style that what is legal and acceptable today may be very illegal 10 or 20 years from now. Staying flexible is a requirement for surviving in the financial markets.

# Notes

## Introduction

1. "Madoff Victims: Gov't Missed Red Flags," CBS News (March 13, 2009), http://wcbstv.com/national/madoff.ponzi.victims.2.957937.html (accessed April 20, 2009).
2. Ibid.
3. Based on a comparison of returns of the S&P 500 Index versus the US 10 Year Government Bond Total Return Index over rolling 20-year periods from 1926 through 2008. Source: Ibbotson Analyst, Copyright 2008, Morningstar Inc.

## Chapter 1: Good Fences Make Good Neighbors

1. Josh Levs, "Authorities: Pilot Who Bailed From Plane Under Securities Probe," CNN.com (January 12, 2009), http://www.cnn.com/2009/US/01/12/florida.plane.crash/ (accessed March 31, 2009).
2. "CFTC Charges Nicholas Cosmo and Agape Companies with Defrauding Customers of Tens of Millions of Dollars in Commodity Futures Trading Scheme," US Commodity Futures Trading Commission (January 27, 2009), http://www.cftc.gov/newsroom/enforcementpressreleases/2009/pr5606-09.html (accessed March 31, 2009).

3. US Securities and Exchange Commission, "SEC Charges Joseph S. Forte for Conducting Multi-Million Dollar Ponzi Scheme" (January 5, 2009), http://www.sec.gov/news/press/2009/2009-5.htm (accessed March 31, 2009).

4. Marc Lacey, "A Last Vanishing Act for Robert Vesco, Fugitive," *New York Times* (May 3, 2008), http://www.nytimes.com/2008/05/03/world/americas/03vesco.html?_r=1&pagewanted=1 (accessed March 31, 2009).

5. "The Collapse of the Kreuger Legend," *The Literary Digest* 113 (May 7, 1932), 36–39; "Why the House of Kreuger Fel," *The Literary Digest* 115 (Feb 4, 1933), 40.

6. See note 2.

7. Securities and Exchange Commission v Arthur Nadel et al., 8:09cv00087-RAL-TBM, (United States District Court Middle District of Florida Tampa Division 2009), http://www.sec.gov/litigation/complaints/2009/comp20858.pdf.

8. Ibid.

9. Securites and Exchange Commission v Robert Brown Jr and Trebor Company et al., 4:08cv03517-CW, case 3517, (United States District Court Northern District of California 2008), http://www.sec.gov/litigation/complaints/2008/comp20653.pdf.

10. Securities and Exchange Commission v Kirk S. Wright et al., 1 06cv0438, (United States District Court for the Northern District of Georgia Atlanta Division 2006), http://sec.gov/litigation/complaints/comp19581.pdf.

11. Securities and Exchange Commission v Amerindo Invetment Advisors Inc et al., (United States District Court Southern District of New York 2005), http://sec.gov/litigation/complaints/comp19245.pdf.

12. Rachael Bell, "Martin Frankel: Sex, Greed, and $200 Million Fraud," TruTV, http://www.trutv.com/library/crime/notorious_murders/classics/frankel/biblio.html (accessed April 2, 2009).

13. "A Century of Ponzi Schemes," *New York Times* (December 15, 2008), http://dealbook.blogs.nytimes.com/2008/12/15/a-century-of-ponzi-schemes/ (accessed April 2, 2009).

14. Diana B. Heriques and Jack Healy, "Madoff Goes to Jail After Guilty Pleas," *New York Times* (March 12, 2009), http://www.nytimes.com/2009/03/13/business/13madoff.html?fta=y (accessed April 2, 2009).

15. Bob Clark, "The Perfect Ponzi," *Investment Advisor* (February 1, 2009), http://www.investmentadvisor.com/Issues/2009/February%202009/Pages/The-Perfect-Ponzi.aspx (accessed April 2, 2009).

16. "Stanford Knighted by Antigua-Barbuda," Caribbean Net News (November 2, 2006), http://www.caribbeannetnews.com/cgi-script/csArticles/articles/000040/004049.htm (accessed April 2, 2009).

17. Securities and Exchange Commission v Stanford International Bank, Ltd. et al., 3-09-CV-0298-N (United States District Court for the Northern District of Texas, Dallas Division), http://www.stanfordfinancialreceivership.com/documents/Interim_Report_Dated_April_23_2009.pdf.

18. Clifford Krauss, "Stanford Points Fingers in Fraud Case," *New York Times* (April 20, 2009) http://www.nytimes.com/2009/04/21/business/21stanford.html?em (accessed April 24, 2009).

19. See note 10.

20. Mike Tierney, "Hedge Fund Manager's Death Does Not Halt Suit Against NFL and Player's Union," *New York Times* (June 2, 2008), http://www.nytimes.com/2008/06/02/sports/football/02wright.html (acccessed April 2, 2009).

21. Securities and Exchange Commission v Frank D. Gruttadauria et al., 1:02CV324, (United States District Court Northern District of Ohio, Eastern Division 2002), http://www.sec.gov/litigation/complaints/complr17369.htm.

22. John Churchill, "Hall of Shame," *Registered Rep* (August 1, 2006), http://registeredrep.com/mag/finance_hall_shame/ (accessed April 2, 2009).

23. See note 21.

## Chapter 2: Too Good to Be True Usually Is

1. US Securities and Exchange Commission, "SEC Charges Joseph S. Forte for Conducting Multi-Million Dollar Ponzi Scheme" (January 5, 2009), http://www.sec.gov/news/press/2009/2009-5.htm (accessed March 31, 2009).

2. US Commodity Futures Trading Commission, "CFTC Charges Nicholas Cosmo and Agape Companies with Defrauding Customers of Tens of Millions of Dollars in Commodity Futures Trading Scheme," (January 27, 2009), http://www.cftc.gov/newsroom/enforcementpressreleases/2009/pr5606-09.html (accessed April 6, 2009).

3. Securities and Exchange Commission v Kirk S. Wright et al., 1 06cv0438, (United States District Court for the Northern District of Georgia Atlanta Division 2006), http://sec.gov/litigation/complaints/comp19581.pdf.

4. Thomson Datastream.

5. Ibid.

6. Roger Parloff, "Madoff 101: Total Immersion for Lawyers," *Fortune* (February 26, 2009), http://money.cnn.com/2009/02/26/news/newsmakers/parloff_madoff.fortune/ (accessed April 6, 2009); Tom Hays, "Trustee: Some Madoff Stock Trades Were Fiction," *USA Today* (February 20, 2009), http://content.usatoday.net/dist/custom/gci/InsidePage.aspx?cId=dailyrecord&sParam=30208657.story (accessed April 7, 2009).

7. David Scheer and Alison Fitzgerald, "Allen Stanford Accused of 'Massive, Ongoing' Fraud," Bloomberg (February 17, 2009), http://www.bloomberg .com/apps/news?pid=20601087&sid=aK6tg..PNMos&refer=home (accessed April 7, 2009); Thomson Datastream.

8. See note 2.

9. Securities and Exchange Commission v Arthur Nadel et al., (U.S. District Court for the Middle District of Florida, Civil Action No. 8:09-CV-00087-RAL-TBM filed January 21, 2009), http://www.sec.gov/litigation/ litreleases/2009/lr20858.htm.

10. Alex Altman, "Ponzi Schemes," *Time* (December 15, 2008), http://www.time .com/time/business/article/0,8599,1866680,00.html (accessed April 7, 2009).

11. Extract of "Quantitative Analysis of Investor Behavior 2008," Dalbar, Inc. 2008.

## Chapter 3: Don't Be Blinded By Flashy Tactics

1. Erin E. Arvedlund, "Don't Ask, Don't Tell," Barron's (May 7, 2001), http://online .barrons.com/article/SB989019667829349012.html (accessed April 20, 2009).

2. Ibid.

3. "What We Wrote About Madoff," Barron's (December 22, 2008), http://online .barrons.com/article/SB122973813073623485.html (accessed April 20, 2009).

4. US Securities and Exchange Commission, "SEC Charges Joseph S. Forte for Conducting Multi-Million Dollar Ponzi Scheme" (January 5, 2009), http:// www.sec.gov/news/press/2009/2009-5.htm (accessed March 31, 2009).

5. Securities and Exchange Commission v Robert Brown, Jr. and Trebor Company et al., 4:08cv03517-CW, case 3517, (United States District Court Northern District of California 2008), http://www.sec.gov/litigation/ complaints/2008/comp20653.pdf; US Securities and Exchange Commission, "SEC Charges Hillsborough, Calif. Investment Adviser With Misappropriating Millions of Dollars From Clients," (July 23, 2008), http://www.sec.gov/ litigation/litreleases/2008/lr20653.htm (accessed April 20, 2009).

6. Ibid.

7. Monée Fields-White, "Kirk Wright's Razzle-Dazzle Play," Bloomberg Markets (October 2006), http://www.bloomberg.com/news/marketsmag/ wright.pdf (accessed April 20, 2009).

8. Stephen Foley, "The Madoff Files: Bernies Billions," Independent (January 30, 2009), http://www.independent.ie/business/world/the-madoff-files-bernies-billions-1620987.html (accessed April 20, 2009).

9. See note 7.

10. See note 3.

11. Ron Chernow, "Madoff and His Models," *New Yorker* (March 23, 2009), http://www.newyorker.com/reporting/2009/03/23/090323fa_fact_chernow (accessed April 20, 2009).

12. "Madoff's Victims," *Wall Street Journal* (March 6, 2009), http://s.wsj.net/public/resources/documents/st_madoff_victims_20081215.html (accessed April 20, 2009).

13. Ibid.

14. Lindsay Fortado, "NYU Lost $24 Million With Madoff; Sues Merkin, Funds," Bloomberg (December 24, 2008), http://www.bloomberg.com/apps/ news?pid=20601087&sid=aTaudmNTkM8E&refer=home (Accessed April 20, 2009).

15. Tiernan Ray, "Living to Tell About Madoff," Barron's (December 22, 2008), http://online.barrons.com/article/SB122971149101722151.html?mod=rss_barrons_electronic_qa (accessed April 20, 2009).

16. Cynthia Cotts, Katherine Burton, Elena Logutenkova, "Credit Suisse Urged Clients to Dump Madoff Funds," Bloomberg (January 7, 2009), http://www.bloomberg.com/apps/news?pid=newsarchive&sid=aLogODm_AZF8 (accessed March 10, 2009).

17. Ibbotson Analyst, Copyright 2008, Morningstar Inc.

18. Rachel Beck, "'Experts' Snowed: Madoff's Scheme Fooled People Who Are Paid to Know Better," *Associated Press* (December 16, 2008).

## Chapter 4: Exclusivity, Marble, and Other Things That Don't Matter

1. Brian Ross and Vic Walter, "Tearful Allen Stanford Expects Indictment in Two Weeks," ABC News (April 6, 2009) http://abcnews.go.com/Blotter/WallStreet/story?id=7270405&page=1 (accessed April 20, 2009).

2. Erin E. Arvedlund, "Don't Ask, Don't Tell," Barron's (May 7, 2001), http://online.barrons.com/article/SB989019667829349012.html (accessed March 31, 2009).

3. Mark Seal, "Madoff's World," *Vanity Fair* (April 2009), http://www.vanityfair.com/politics/features/2009/04/madoff200904 (accessed March 31, 2009).

4. Gary Dymski and Thomas Maier, "LI Victims of Madoff: 'He Has No Conscience,'" *Newsday* (March 12, 2009), http://www.newsday.com/services/newspaper/printedition/thursday/business/ny-bzside0313,0,5048879.story (accessed March 31, 2009).

5. Jesse Westbrook, David Scheer, and Mark Pittman, "Madoff Tipster Markopolos Cites SEC's 'Ineptitude,'" Bloomberg (February 4, 2009), http://www.bloomberg.com/apps/news?pid=newsarchive&sid=a_UBDG13Gld0 (accessed March 31, 2009).

6. Bob Clark, "The Perfect Ponzi," Investment Advisor (February 1, 2009), http://www.investmentadvisor.com/Issues/2009/February%202009/Pages/The-Perfect-Ponzi.aspx (accessed March 31, 2009).

7. James B. Stewart, "The Opera Lover," *New Yorker* (February 13, 2006).

8. Tom Leonard, "Opera Patron Alberto Vilar Convicted of Fraud and Money Laundering," *The Telegraph* (November 21, 2008), http://www.telegraph.co.uk/news/worldnews/northamerica/usa/3493101/Opera-patron-Alberto-Vilar-convicted-of-fraud-and-money-laundering.html (accessed March 31, 2009).

9. Lawrence Delevingne, "Stanford Financial: How To Buy A Reputation," CNN Money (March 4, 2009), http://money.cnn.com/2009/03/04/news/newsmakers/stanford_influence.fortune/index.htm?postversion=2009030412 (accessed March 31, 2009).

10. Eugenia Levenson, "One Madoff Charity Goes Unscathed," CNN Money (December 17,2008), http://money.cnn.com/2008/12/17/news/companies/madoff_lymphoma.fortune/index.htm (accessed March 31, 2009).

11. "Madoff's Victims," *Wall Street Journal* (March 6, 2009), http://s.wsj.net/public/resources/documents/st_madoff_victims_20081215.html (accessed April 20, 2009).

12. Amanda Carpenter, "Madoff Spent Nearly $1 Million Lobbying and on Democratic Causes," *Washington Times* (March 13, 2009), http://washingtontimes.com/weblogs/back-story/2009/Mar/13/madoff-spent-nearly-1-million-lobbying-and-democra/ (accessed March 31, 2009).

13. See note 9.

14. Robert L. Fitzpatrick, "Utah Legislature Passes Pyramid Scheme 'Safe Harbor' Amendments," MLM Watch (March 1, 2006), http://www.mlmwatch.org/11Legal/utahbill.html (accessed March 31, 2009).

15. See note 3.

16. Monee Fields-White, "Kirk Wright's Razzle-Dazzle Play," Bloomberg Markets (October 2006), http://www.bloomberg.com/news/marketsmag/wright.pdf (accessed April 20, 2009).

17. FT Reporters, "Stanford's Sugar-Crusted Show," *Financial Times* (March 3,2009), http://www.ft.com/cms/s/0/be1a1c12-0825-11de-8a33-0000779fd2ac,dwp_uuid=d7b5a5de-07de-11de-8a33-0000779fd2ac.html?nclick_check=1 (accessed March 31, 2009).

18. "Stanford Eagle 2008," *Stanford Financial*, http://www.stanfordfinancial.com/Magazine/Stanford_Eagle.pdf (accessed March 31, 2009).

19. Matthew Goldstein, "Stanford's Rocky Start," *BusinessWeek* (March 4, 2009), http://www.businessweek.com/bwdaily/dnflash/content/mar2009/db2009033_601499.htm?chan=top+news_top+news+index+-+temp_top+story (accessed March 31, 2009).

20. James B. Stewart, "The Opera Lover," *New Yorker* (February 13, 2006).
21. See note 17.

## Chapter 5: Due Diligence Is Your Job, No One Else's

1. US Securities and Exchange Commission, "SEC Files Complaint Against Daren L. Palmer and Trigon Group for Operating a $40 million Ponzil Scehem and Obtains Orders Freezing Assets, and Appointing a Reciever," (February 27, 2009), http://www.sec.gov/litigation/litreleases/2009/lr20918.htm (accessed April 24, 2009).

2. Clifford Krauss, "Stanford Points Fingers in Fraud Case," *New York Times* (April 20, 2009), http://www.nytimes.com/2009/04/21/business/21stanford.html?em (accessed April 24, 2009).

3. Matthew Goldstein, "Stanford's Rocky Start," *BusinessWeek* (March 4, 2009), http://www.businessweek.com/bwdaily/dnflash/content/mar2009/db2009033_601499.htm?chan=top+news_top (accessed March 31, 2009).

4. Stanford Eagle 2008, *Stanford Financial*, http://www.stanfordfinancial.com/Magazine/Stanford_Eagle.pdf (accessed March 31, 2009).

5. See note 3.

6. Zachary A. Goldfarb, "Probe of Stanford Began at Least 3 Years Ago," *Washington Post* (February 21, 2009), http://www.washingtonpost.com/wp-dyn/content/article/2009/02/20/AR2009022003420.html (accessed March 31, 2009).

7. Sue Asci and Jed Horowitz, "RIAs Angry Over SEC Move to Contact Clients Directly," *Investment News* (March 12, 2009), http://www.investmentnews.com/apps/pbcs.dll/article?AID=/20090312/REG/903129989/1032 (accessed April 21, 2009).

8. Ross Kerber, "The Whistleblower," *Boston Globe* (January 8, 2009), http://www.boston.com/business/articles/2009/01/08/the_whistleblower/?page=1 (accessed March 31, 2009).

9. Bob Clark, "The Perfect Ponzi," *Investment Advisor* (February 1, 2009), http://www.investmentadvisor.com/Issues/2009/February%202009/Pages/The-Perfect-Ponzi.aspx (accessed March 29, 2009).

10. Robert Chew, "Bernie Madoff's Victims: Why Some Have No Recourse," *Time* (January 12, 2009), http://www.time.com/time/business/article/0,8599,1871173,00.html (accessed March 31, 2009).

11. "Madoff's Victims," *Wall Street Journal* (March 6, 2009), http://s.wsj.net/public/resources/documents/st_madoff_victims_20081215.html (accessed March 31, 2009).

12. Ibid.

13. Dunstant Prial, "Madoff Feeder Fund Charged with Fraud in Mass," FoxBusiness (April 1, 2009), http://www.foxbusiness.com/story/markets/market-overview/madoff-feeder-fund-charged-fraud-mass/ (accessed April 21, 2009).

14. Robert Frank and Peter Lattman, "Cohmad Securities Subpoenaed Over Relationship With Firm," *Wall Street Journal* (December 17, 2008), http://online.wsj.com/article/SB122948051697212935.html (accessed April 24, 2008).

15. See note 11.

16. Jane Musgrave, "Scandal Sullies Robert Jaffe as Feds Probe Ties to Bernard Madoff," *Palm Beach Post* (December 20, 2008), http://www.palmbeachpost.com/localnews/content/local_news/epaper/2008/12/20/a1a_jaffe_1221.html (accessed March 31, 2009).

17. Monée Fields-White, "Kirk Wright's Razzle-Dazzle Play," Bloomberg Markets (October 2006), http://www.bloomberg.com/news/marketsmag/wright.pdf (accessed April 21, 2009).

18. "Madoff Auditor Charged With Securities Fraud," *Journal of Accountancy* (March 19, 2009), http://www.journalofaccountancy.com/Web/20091553 (accessed May 5, 2009).

19. Stephanie Bodoni, "UBS, Accounting Firm Sued Over Fund Linked to Madoff," Bloomberg (March 19, 2009), http://www.bloomberg.com/apps/news?pid=20601087&sid=a6Gvh2RgyMFU&dbk (accessed March 31, 2009).

20. Ron Chernow, "Madoff and His Models," *New Yorker* (March 23, 2009), http://www.newyorker.com/reporting/2009/03/23/090323fa_fact_chernow (accessed April 21, 2009).

21. James Quinn, "'Generous' Bernard Madoff Was Obsessed With Cleaning, Recalls Employee," *Telegraph* (March 24, 2009), http://www.telegraph.co.uk/finance/financetopics/bernard-madoff/5039591/Generous-Bernard-Madoff-was-obsessed-with-cleaning-recalls-employee.html (accessed March 31, 2009).

## Chapter 6: A Financial Fraud–Free Future

1. Robert Cookson, Michael Peel, and Joanna Chung, "SEC Alerted About Stanford in 2003," *Financial Times* (February 27, 2009), http://www.ft.com/cms/s/0/148817be-043b-11de-845b-000077b07658.html?nclick_check=1 (accessed April 20, 2009).

# Index

# About the Authors

**Ken Fisher** is best known for his prestigious "Portfolio Strategy" column in *Forbes* magazine, where his twenty-five-year tenure of high-profile calls makes him the fourth longest-running columnist in *Forbes'* 90-plus-year history. Ken is the founder, Chairman, and CEO of Fisher Investments, an independent global money management firm. He is on *Investment Advisor* magazine's prestigious IA-25 list of the industry's most influential people; is the award-winning author of numerous scholarly articles; and has published five previous books, including the *New York Times* bestsellers *The Only Three Questions That Count* and *The Ten Roads to Riches*—both of which are published by Wiley. Ken has been published, interviewed, and/or appeared in most major American, British, and German finance or business periodicals. He has a weekly column in *Focus Money*, Germany's leading weekly finance magazine.

**Lara Hoffmans** graduated from the University of Notre Dame with a BA in theatre. She is a content manager at Fisher Investments and contributing editor of MarketMinder.com. She also coauthored with Ken Fisher the bestsellers *The Only Three Questions That Count* and *The Ten Roads to Riches*.